U2
IN THE NAME OF LOVE

A History from Ireland's Hot Press Magazine

Edited by Niall Stokes

HARMONY BOOKS
NEW YORK

Edited by Niall Stokes
with Liam Mackey

Designed by Ian McColl
Cover Pic: Colm Henry
Hand Colouring by Amelia Stein

Contributors:
Bill Graham
Jackie Hayden
Neil McCormick
Declan Lynch
Dermot Stokes
and all the staff at Hot Press

Production Co-ordination: Mairin Sheehy

Published in the United States in 1986 by
Harmony Books, a division of Crown Publishers, Inc., 225 Park Avenue South, New York, NY 10003
and simultaneously in Canada by
General Publishing Company Limited

First published in Ireland as
The U2 File
by Hot Press, 22 Wicklow Street, Dublin 2

HARMONY and colophon are trademarks of
Crown Publishers, Inc.

Manufactured in Ireland

Library of Congress Cataloging-in-Publication Data
Main entry under title:

U2 : in the name of love.

Originally published: The U2 file. Dublin, Ireland : Hot Press, 1985.
1. U2 (Musical group) 2. Rock musicians -- Ireland -- Biography. I. Stokes, Niall. II. Hot press.
ML421.U2U2 1986   784.5'4'00922 [B]   85-27212
ISBN 0-517-56215-4 (pbk.)

10 9 8 7 6 5 4 3 2 1

First American Edition

Special thanks: To Adam, Larry, Bono and the Edge, not just for the magnificent music but for the
friendship and inspiration.
To Paul McGuinness for all his support.
To Rob Partridge and everyone at Island for the pictures and for an all-round exceptional press service.
To Neil Storey for keeping the faith.
To Anton Corbijn, Adrian Boot, miscellaneous photographers — and especially to Colm Henry for his brilliant
pictures down the years.
To Mairin Sheehy for the work that goes uncredited.
To Jackie Hayden for more than can be expressed.
To Paul Hourihane and Ken Hutton for wheeling and dealing.
To Ian McColl for working his ass off.
To Fiona Looney and Damien Corless for valiant proofreading.
To Jonathan Wells, Fred Schruers, Ted Schwarz and Maurice Behan in the US of A.
To Ann-Louise and everyone at Windmill, Ossie Kilkenny, Jim Aiken, Steve Rapid, Willie Kavanagh
and Tony Mangan
To all the staff at Hot Press, past and present.
And finally to Liam Mackey for the comradeship
and to Bill Graham — for being there first.

U2

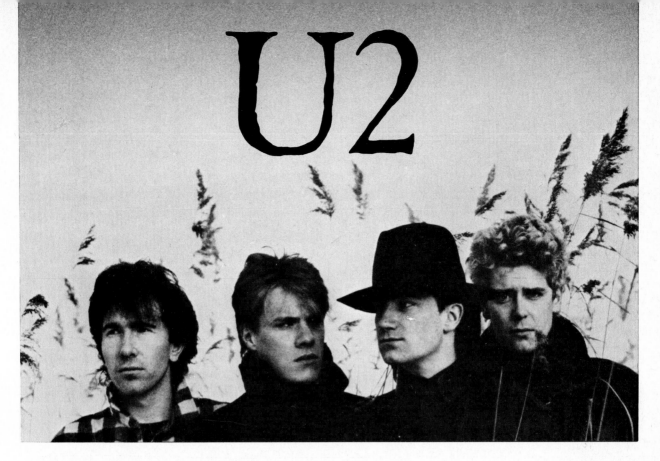

THIS BOOK, these pictures, these words, tell the U2 story.

They tell it with innocence rather than hindsight, in the language of the time rather than that of history: this is a record of the triumphant-present in the making, the documentary of a band on the run, breaking lap records, surprising itself, surpassing itself, and ultimately turning silver into gold into platinum before our very eyes. But even that magnificent feat of alchemy is so much less than the magic they wrought in their music ...

From the beginning, U2 inspired faith. How and why is explained in different ways by different writers whom their magic touched in those early days but on that critical point, there was an extraordinary unanimity. The band radiated a sense of vision, a sense of destiny, even as a fledgling four-piece from Mount Temple, which they never lost in the intervening seven years of constant challenge.

And just as U2 inspired faith, they also inspired care. The depth of their commitment demanded reciprocation. In that light, whatever doubts assailed us – or them? – proved purely transient. They may have made mistakes, they may have over-reached or under-achieved, but their fundamental righteousness of purpose could never be called into question. Where others in rock 'n' roll who had begun in a blinding fire of idealism became inevitably tainted with the cynicism, the tiredness and then the sheer apathy that so ritualistically follows success, U2 refused to allow their spirit to be drained. With a resoluteness that to this day remains a source of wonderment, they have retained the naked honesty that is the core of their music and their identity.

Perhaps art, even more than life, is but a tissue of falsehoods and deception. Perhaps U2, among their peers, simply know best how to dissemble. Perhaps all those well-meaning songs of love and faith and tenderness and optimism and desire – those songs of fire and pride and celebration – are just a massive put-on.

Perhaps, but I don't think so. Because those of us who have been lucky enough to see the band grow almost from birth, who've known the members of U2 well enough personally to be able

5

to relate the music to the people, will find no difficulty in reconciling the two. It comes back to a simple word, but one of momentous significance. The crucial connecting thread which links the different strands in this remarkable story, from rough beginnings in 1978 to heady successes in 1985, is integrity.

Can we have integrity and lose it? Or is it merely that some of us can fool ourselves, even our audience, for just so long before finally realising that it wasn't worth the effort, that in any event it's more profitable to pander? Whatever the truth about that, it is a hallmark of their enduring greatness that U2 have not reneged, have not lowered their sights, have not corrupted their values, have not abandoned the aspirations which fired that first inspirational D-chord.

Of course you're right. Integrity is a fine thing but then why aren't you a star? To be artistically successful takes talent, and creativity and determination and hard work — not to mention the ability to tune an oul' guitar. Throw in sound management, the right record company and a smattering of good luck and you're getting close to defining the ingredients that have combined to make this band what they are. But ultimately, to make great music requires something special, something transcendent, and the overwhelming evidence in this definitive collection of U2 interviews, reviews, critiques, confessions and dissertations from the pages of Hot Press, is that Adam, Bono, Larry and the Edge had it from the start. They have made great music, and, at bottom, *that's* why they're worth all the love and care and attention that their fans have lavished on them these past seven years and more ...

We hope those same fans will relish this blow by blow account, as it happened, of the rise and rise of the greatest Irish rock band of all ...

Niall Stokes

Hot Press is a rock magazine published fortnightly and is available on subscription from Hot Press, 22 Wicklow Street, Dublin 2, Ireland.

Yep! It's U2

U2, 1978 (l to r): Paul Hewson (aka Bono Vox), Dave Evans (aka The Edge), Larry Mullen and Adam Clayton.

Bill Graham introduces a promising new Dublin four-piece.

Another contender for the titles vacated by The Rats and The Radiators, U-2 arrive on the scene with some highly influential supporters. With Steve Rapid acting as mentor, (though not manager) and interest from CBS, the north-side band have made early progress before even venturing into the better-known centre-city gigs. Their recent rise to new-found prominence is due to a victory in an *Evening Press*/Harp Lager talent contest.

Normally, such contests are ho-hum cabaret affairs but Jackie Hayden from CBS was one of the judges and was sufficiently impressed to pay for a short demo session in Keystone, which is where I caught up with them.

I must report that it wasn't the happiest of sessions, the band's inexperience showing up on what was a rush job. Their first numbers were their latest songs which suffered as they were still getting the measure of themselves and the studio. It wasn't till later on that their real potential came through.

U-2 describe themselves as purveyors of New Wave pop although they're wise enough to avoid the now deceased power-pop tag. However, they've also got hard-rock leanings, not surprisingly since they used to concentrate on that music when they went under their earlier name as The Hype. To their credit, they don't disguise that background.

To their credit again, U-2 are a young band in their last year at school. They impress as articulate, aware and hard-working individuals who are prepared to weigh up others' advice as they embark on their vocation. U2 talk like they intend to be professionals, a primary asset in the battle for recognition. All these qualities and their youth make U-2 a band for the future and one with the attitude to grow and evolve fast.

Since they're currently studying for their Leaving Certs., U-2 won't be immediately around for inspection and further examination for another month or two. Even so, they're encouraging evidence that the flow of young bands hasn't dried up. Who's next? You, three. ■

Bill Graham
Vol. 1 No. 23. April 28th. 1978

U2 in statuesque pose. Pic: Bernard Farrell

U2 Could Be a Headline

U2 declare their intentions to Bill Graham

It started with a telephone call — to be more accurate a barrage of such communications — from U-2's bassist Adam Clayton, part of a prolonged campaign that eventually dragged me out of house and home across the river to meet with members of the band. I hadn't seen them play but I was aware they'd won some sort of a band competition in Limerick, an achievement sufficient to impel me to negotiate the cross-town traffic but hardly the ultimate seal of approval given the doubtful merits of Irish music competitions.

Which is where it all began. Frankly, this can't be unbiased judicial journalism. I happen to be a fan of U-2, believing them to be a group of very special talents. But trying to retain some sense of semi-detachment, I've got to reckon with the possibility that I've been snowed by my own self-hype. Moreover, in the small world of Irish rock, roles get duplicated. Besides being a fan, one ends up as some species of friend and adviser with all the self-involvement that entails — in my case to the point of making the connection that lined them up with their manager, Paul McGuinness. You can understand my credit's on the line.

As I repeat, I hadn't heard them play. But that first encounter brought me face to face with a foursome who had a precociousness, open-mindedness and willingness to learn that was unusual among Irish bands I'd met heretofore, a demeanour that implied that if their musical abilities were anyway comparable to their personality, U-2 were a band worth keeping a line open to.

First playing impressions were favourable but not immediately sufficient to lift them unchallengingly above the ruck of bands wandering around last summer. It wasn't 'till the Autumn that U-2 began to implant themselves indelibly in my consciousness.

The last six months of '78 were depressing. Very little energy was being generated, the first Dublin wave — the Vipers, Sacre Bleu, Revolver, Fit Kilkenny and The Remoulds — all passing through a phase of re-assessment and examination of their rock consciences to

some extent. Satisfaction wasn't easily to be found.

U-2 increasingly came to fill that gap. Part of it was due to their exuberance — U-2 have a vaulting unclouded optimism that's very special — a virtue all the more welcome given the misanthropic weather that was reaching us from London, a mood that I didn't react to equably. Yet aside from any similarity of temperament, U-2 were a band whose basic direction was set and on course, whose playing capacity was consistently evolving and whose songs both provided new vistas at each hearing and were unfussed by trends above or beneath them. They delivered when I needed it and I can't say more.

They started as a band at Mount Temple, a five-piece that also included Dave Edge's brother Dik (on second guitar), who left them for the Virgin Prunes when they settled for a four-piece line-up. They weren't called U-2 then, instead initially christening themselves the Hype, a title later ditched because they felt it out of line with the times. None of the others had been in a band except bassist Adam Clayton who had been with the Max Quad Band, an aggregation that then included George Sweeney, current guitarist with the Vipers.

It wasn't as if they began programmed with the intention of taking on the world. Rather one gig and contact led to another, the victory in the Limerick band competition bringing them to the attention of CBS's Jackie Hayden who had been a judge, and he consequently took them into Keystone Studios for a demo session. A hurried runthrough, it wasn't to their liking and although all credit to Hayden for his perceptive scouting, the encounter was premature given the band's development since.

A contract was vaguely mooted but U-2 weren't taking up any options and the nine months since Limerick have found them concentrating on refining their abilities, undertaking an apprenticeship that along the way has gained them support slots with both the Stranglers and The Greedy Bastards. But their most convincing performances have been in McGonagles — the band played an early Autumn date with Revolver that gained them the esteem of both Johnny Fingers and Phil

Bono

Pic: Colm Henry.

Bono

Pic: Colm Henry.

Chevron, I pick their *Hot Press* party date and manager Paul McGuinness selects an early January performance — yet each gig had the appearance of a young band flexing and exercising their wings before taking the flight from the nest. But Adam Clayton may have the wisest word when he says "We're only now getting the feel of our identity".

Certainly, U-2 are ready, teetering on the verge of a recording contract. A second and more settled demo session was overseen in December by Barry Devlin with superior results and for once a band's self-confident impatience is equalled by their achievements. If their emergence has been slower than Dublin bands of an equivalent age, it's partially due to the caution of McGuinness whose management philosophy downplays the importance of Irish status during a band's adolescence — i.e. spray-cans do not a hit-act make, emphasising instead a band's capacity to be judged by their international potential and not by their position among their local peers.

The point is to be satisfied by nothing less than the best and U-2's values veer towards the same perfectionism. Thus, they've decided to remodel the set they've been peddling these last six months, a brave undertaking given its undeniable quality. Explains vocalist Bono. "We're now working on a new set that's more visual. We'll be using a projector and tapes and rewriting and rearranging some of the songs and bringing new ones in".

They will agree that the decision is partly due to interaction with their allies, The Virgin Prunes, Bono believing that there's a need for an inversion of roles in that "The Prunes were concentrating on the visual, non-musical things and now they must come to grips with the music, while we've got to learn from their stage things, now that we're confident about our music."

That relationship of mentors and fans has undergone a partial reversal, The Prunes' rise to infancy latterly tending to eclipse U-2, a foible of fortune that both parties will admit has led to some stresses, albeit now healed. My own hunch is their functions and futures are destined to diverge, run through a circle before both return to meet again.

"It's to bring people up and bring people down, an emotional force in which we want to combine energy, power, sensitivity and depth" — thus spake Bono on the musical intent of these new romantics and he expands by saying their new set will be designed to accentuate both the highs and lows with slower songs brought in for the purpose. U-2 don't believe in pandering to the hi-speed pogo.

A conscientious publicist might feel obliged to line U-2 up among the New Wave, but the only props he'd have for such a scam would be their youth and its attendant vitality. Yet, if the first punk manifestos are interpreted to include both these values and also music that's not easily categorisable, then U-2 fit the bill.

Unlike any Irish band of the last three years, their debts are difficult to expose. Yes, they are a tempestuous three-piece with a power-pack vocalist driven to dominate the audience — but beyond that, their songs travel on their own tails. Adam Clayton says "We want to be trend-setters, not trend-followers." And for once, that ill-used cliche is true.

We do reach one moment of unanimity when I assert that their songs written by Dave and Bono, with the latter as co-ordinator and quality controller, are an extension and crystallisation of the most positive aspects of pre-punk 70's rock, exposed through the hypercritical microscope of the last three years and all the better for it.

Such might seem a paradox. It needn't be. One doesn't need to inhabit blackmail corner to know that the disruptors of class '76 have a more complex musical history than their early bios made out. Moreover, it could be argued that many punks — particularly the imposters of the 25 and over variety — were unoriginally sticking to the brief and blueprint put out by the Press.

So many diverse influences nestle among the music of the leading creators and like them U-2 have formed their own synthesis, a brand of light metal stripped of excess and redundant posturing — Paul McGuinness claims a major characteristic is "their avoidance of waste" — that believes that aggressive guitar-rock can be mated to melodic invention and freed from (a) ludicrous Judas Priest/Queen football chants (b) clumsy drag-down R 'n' B cliche-a-boogie and (c) flashy but shallow techno-rock. And that'll suffice for now.

Besides the constructions, there are the emotions and the themes. "Our songs are about different aspects, maybe spiritual", Bono says, "because every teenager, every youth does experience spiritual things, like going to church — do you agree with that? See, I have problems about it — things like girls, sex. But we're also dealing with spiritual questions, ones which few groups ever touch even if I know that teenagers do think about these matters."

U-2 u-c aren't interested in gang-bangs, New York pimps, whips and furs, high-fashion queens or indeed the imminent British counter-revolution. Bono's testimony is that after acne comes anguish, songs about backseat-lovemaking scenes at 16 which are substituted for by wider spiritual insecurities at 18. It's an angle midway betwen Kate Bush and Paul Weller — and unequivocally I refer to both because they and U-2 are not the same generation as Bob Geldof or Joe Strummer — and perhaps the source of U-2's greatest fascination

Bono. Pic: Bernard Farrell

or flaw, I can't decide which.

U-2 are unmarked by sin, exuberant because they retain innocence. Rock has so many lurking demons, in both its temptations and its traps that a band find themselves inexorably impelled towards the devil's party (who, of course, has the best songs!). U-2's determination and dedication could be a necessary shield; it also could bar them from the Faustian forces that generate rock's dreams as much as its nightmares.

Somehow, I don't believe U-2's future will be among the more predictable. They have the originality and vivacity to make their own especial contribution to Irish rock. But that lack of derivativeness means they could have translation problems in Britain. U-2 represent a refining of traditional 70's rock modes, a policy that might find their freshness and spontaneity mistaken for conservatism by those unprepared to listen long enough. Strangely, they may be more accessible to American ears, a factor that activates my second fear in that the band could, if not delicately handled, fall between two continents and be drowned on the Atlantic crossing.

U-2 are honourable and being honourable could lack mystique. It's an honesty Bono might claim as the source of their identity. On their live performances, he says — "When I'm annoyed, I show it. When that feedback arrived at the Project, I started showing my anger and growling. And people say he's getting annoyed and I show it. The same when it's happening right, then I smile and it means so much to me and I want to keep everything for everybody. But the other hand of it is being annoyed which is also unprofessional" — comments indicative of the link between capability and poselessness he proposes to tread. Later he'll say that he often feels "like an offering to an audience".

Adam Clayton can summarise the second U-2 theme that musicianship and youth aren't antagonistic — "We're trying to prove that we are credible. Too many people say you're just young punks, wait till you're about 30 like Bob Dylan or someone." This convert wants to believe him. Others may be sought as secondary Thin Lizzies and Boomtown Rats but U-2's expression owes no debts. I'm tired of listening to demo tapes, I want that record.■ **Bill Graham. Vol 2 No. 19 March 8 1979**

U2 Treats U

Declan Lynch sees U2 play Dublin's Dandelion Green.

T HE TENSION around Malahide must be palpable these days; it's working, for God's sake, it's working! The project which began so ignominiously in the lives of four ambitious middle class kiddies has developed through a plethora of errors, hiccups, pratfalls, accusations, stupidities, and barely-savoured successes, into a movement.

They've come from Killiney and Foxrock, and also Cabra and Raheny to be here today, and they've come to *dance*, mister — and *sing*, and *participate* and only maybe evaluate. What's more, they've dressed up with **an unmistakable detail.** If U2 are playing, there's no knowing who might be there, right?

Most important is the fact that U-2 kiddies are actually *young*. What with The Skids and Police and Gen. X doing the round on every turntable in the civilised world, Paddy pop kids have decided that Paul, Dave, Adam and Larry (for it is they) are cooler than death and more than just another *young band*. U-2 are now the mentors, even father figures (gaspo!), for a new generation of attempted rises to popularity and Juke Box Jury appearances, and they haven't even released a record. Very strange indeed.

I thought this was a great gig. Admittedly there are easier places to play than Dandelion Green — the Black Hole of Calcutta being the one which springs to mind with greatest facility.

But obstacles mean nothing to these boys now, or so it seems. They're making everything into momentum,

1979. U2 play one of their legendary Dandelion Green gigs. Pic: Colm Henry.

turning it into gravy, and they'll probably be in your town this week. U-2 have frankly gigged their butts off to be as tight and effective as their excellent set continues to indicate. When Paul Hewson, once a prat, now the frontman he's always wanted to be, sprays "U-2" in black on the back wall, he's being deliberate, and everyone knows it. Complete conviction and mastery of technique are slowly becoming his, and he doesn't have to bluff anymore. He is *in control,* and you just know that he's been in front of more mirrors than "Jimmy" "Smith" has "hot" "licks" to "play".

Their greatest strength, though, is in the songs, which now vindicate all the occasional obnoxiousness. "Out of Control", "In Your Hand", "Concentration Cramp", "Shadows In Tall Trees", "Judith", and "The Fool" will land them the record contract which, when it comes will be richly deserved, if only for courage and tenacity in the face of such a volume of criticism from the very start. But then, the best are always the most envied, which may be close to the root of things.

Dave Edge is a superlative guitarist and he'll improve so much, being so young, being so bright, so good.

Someday soon, Adam Clayton will wake up and find that he's Phil Lynott, which will please him fully. They've learnt and learnt, honing all those influences (Bowie, even Lizzy to name two) so caringly. Where others are inspired by the same people, U-2 have gone that crucial stage further, and created a unique identifiable sound of their own. It's a good sound, one that's adding nuances to pop and metal, without being either one exclusively. The dark voice whispering market penetration into my ear is being ignored, but out in Malahide, they're probably crapping over it.

Nah, I didn't mean it to sound snide or nasty. That's gone on too long, much too long, because no matter what band you play with south of the border, U-2 can piddle all over you, lucrative publishing deals or not.

Church of Ireland rock 'n' roll knocked me out on a Saturday afternoon, and the metal pop kids say: "it's U-2 for that special treat", Goodnight. ∎

Declan Lynch
Vol. 3 No. 6 August 31st 1979

15

back when: Bono and Susan Moylett of Dublin's now defunct No Romance boutique model new wave fashions.

U2 in the limelight. Pic: Hugo McGuinness

Boys in Control

U2's first Hot Press cover interview. By Niall Stokes.

U2

Pic: Anton Corbijn.

The word is out that U-2 are the band. An amalgam of four school-friends who obviously had something special from the start, such has been the consistency and the speed of their development that they now stand on the brink of an international breakthrough, at an average age of less than nineteen.

In the meantime, to keep the home fires burning while they make their play for the role of the country's foremost rock act — creatively as well as commercially — they have been signed to a three-year deal for Ireland by CBS, a contract which will stand irrespective of international developments. Module one of the ultimate U-2 recorded canon has also been launched onto the local market, in a sufficient variety of sizes and wrappings to satisfy the most fetishistic of collectors: as an initial statement of intent, it stands with the best local records ever. Its crucial strength is its startling uniqueness: you have never heard anything before to which "Out Of Control" or "Boy/Girl" or "Stories for Boys" can be remotely reliably compared.

Because U-2 are a band who have meticulously and conscientiously avoided the trap of being out of control, a paradoxical condition attendant on the common initial error of plugging into a limited musical frame of reference. They are not punk. They are not pop. They are not glam. They are not "metal", let alone heavy. They are hardly country!

> **U2 are potentially great because their music is informed with a depth of concern for things and people and ideas. Which is, at the best of times, anything but commonplace.**

Not that they are blind to what is going on around them. Unlike more "temperamental" musicians, utterly precious about the notion that they are creative and original people and inordinately suspicious of the suggestion that they might have listened to someone else, U-2 will talk freely about "their influences", who they've picked up on individually or collectively — the most certain barometer of the fact that they are *not* significantly indebted to anyone.

There is a basis for this in their creative rationale. Ironically again, it's because they are willing to relinquish control, because they are prepared to fall back on intuition and the power of the subconscious in writing their music, and their lyrics, that the end-result is so distinctive. You know hearing U-2's music that it is intimately personal, that it reflects — with all the inevitable implicit tensions this involves — the personalities, the concerns and the convictions of its perpetrators.

U-2 are good because the band comprises four intelligent, musical people who are also not only willing but anxious to work towards the form of self-fulfilment making rock 'n' roll music entails. U-2 are potentially *great* because they care, because their music is informed with a depth of concern for things and people and ideas. Which is, at the best of times, anything but commonplace.

They are young and naive and above all committed. Not to anything outside themselves which they have yet to grasp either emotionally or intellectually but, simply, to making their contribution. They have maintained what amounts to a foolishly idealistic stance in the face of much cynicism, abuse and, latterly, even sporadic violence. But that foolishness, which is in fact at the very heart of their identity is about to be repaid one hundred times. The fact that they were prepared to go out on to a limb is admirable, the fact that they were prepared to look "silly" in the short term to develop something more powerful in the long run, a sign of their real humility, and the fact that it's all coming together, a perfect form of poetic justice.

And yet they are young enough for it all to come terribly unstuck.

There are five people sitting in (and out) on an interview which extends for over two hours and contains more weight per minute than the vast majority of shorter conversations. The members of the band, Bono (vocals), Adam Clayton (bass), Dave Edge (guitar) and Larry Mullen (drums) are here, as is manager Paul McGuinness, who makes sporadic contributions mainly on matters of business.

THE GENESIS OF A BAND AND ITS PERSONALITY

"People tend to forget that this is a group — like an old fashioned group ..." — Paul McGuinness

Larry: "Getting together in high school, none of us had been in bands before except Adam who was in the Max Quad Band". Dave: "We were all terrible. We just

Dave Edge and Bono check their debut single sleeve. Pic: Hugo McGuinness

couldn't play other people's material — that's how we started writing. We learnt to play by learning how to do our own songs.

Bono: "Adam pretended he could play and used words like "gig" and talked about things like "action" on the bass and we thought 'this is a guy who can play! He was a liar. He actually couldn't play a note. Dave was just playing away on the acoustic and people just kept on coming up and saying "there's something wrong" and we couldn't figure out what it was until suddenly we thought — it's Adam! Adam can't play.

"He (Adam) has had his own distinctive style from the start — at first it was called BLUFF (general laughter) but then it began to work. And he has a different sense of rhythm. You know the story about Jimi Hendrix when he went to a guitar tutor, they told him "forget it — you'll never play guitar, your rhythm's all wrong —" Adam had the same thing. He was fired from the Max Quad Band because he couldn't play bass. Put him on the spot and say play that and he won't, he'll play it his own way. And because of his odd sense of rhythm, he began to develop lines that weren't normal, they weren't cliched . They were good.

"The first song that we played was Stagalee-type

Larry Mullen. Pic: Hugo McGuinness.

funk rock. It was bloody good. I'll tell you how I wrote it. I was just playing the guitar, making the nice sounds of these chords and suddenly there was emotion! It was very definitely "Ooh! this is nice" and then playing more and more and it came like that. And I reckon it still holds good today. We were thinking of offering it to Stagalee."

Dave: "That's when I became a lead guitarist, during that song. I had been playing my guitar for three months and we had this garage guitarist down who was very good — fast and all that — and after seeing him and hearing Paul (Bono) play that riff ... that was it.

"I learned mainly by playing nothing in particular, just fiddling around on top of records."

Bono: "Dave was definitely showing talent very fast. He came down — you know that famous group Mushroom (chorus: No! Cromwell) ... Cromwell ... you know that track "Guinness Rock" has a bit *diddle diddle diddle diddle, diddle diddle diddle diddle*" — Dave came down and said "listen to this" and proceeded to play it. At that stage I wanted to play lead guitar but I couldn't do that. And I still can't.

Dave: "I started off by being influenced by everybody but the only records that I had were borrowed from Fergus across the road and they were Rory Gallagher records."

Bono: "So we began to feed him records — like Marquee Moon."

Dave: "I developed — just generally being told "that's - horrible — do something else". And I would, out of embarrassment. Also listening to other guitarists, like Tom Verlaine."

Bono: "It wasn't my choice to stop playing guitar. About eighteen months ago, they first of all stopped me playing guitar — and I decided I'd be a singer — and then rumours had it that maybe I shouldn't sing. At that stage, I nearly faced — EXIT! But I was the mechanic of the band. I got very frustrated at times — I was always the guy bringing in records and making them listen to them. I eventually stumbled on singing, through a sore throat.

Larry: "I started off five years ago doing military drumming and from there, I had this style of *having* to fill in. I went to other teachers and then to Johnny Wadham and he was teaching me to play jazz. When the band formed, they thought I was great because I was able to fill in. But as it developed, they started to say "try not to put so many rolls in" — and it's only lately that I've managed to cut back. I used to be able to do drum solos — but I can't anymore ..."

By this stage, the instrumental prowess of the individual members of U-2 can hardly be in question. Not yet utterly professional and adaptable musicians in the old school — by any means — each has however developed a proficiency, musicality and personal style which works excellently in the context of the group sound. There is no "obvious weakness", though not every move is inspired and there is always a possibility of individual shakiness. The collective progress from their novice beginnings is, nevertheless, remarkable.

MOMENTS OF SUCCESS
MOMENTS OF RESISTANCE
AND MOMENTS OF RESILIENCE

Bono: "We're not ashamed of how bad we were, 'cos we played this competition in Limerick Civic Week — and we won it on *a spark*. We went down there and we went out on stage — and it had an atmosphere even when we couldn't really play. We just felt good on stage.

"It's hard to define — we went out there and played and Jackie Hayden of CBS, who was a judge in the competition, could see the spark. There were groups like the East Coast Angels and Room Service — who were very proficient musicians — and blew us off in terms of sound but we still won.

"I remember one of our early gigs in a little, tiny Church Hall in Howth. We had two sets — an original set and an unoriginal set. We played the unoriginal set first and then the original one to show people — you see, this is what we do ourselves. For this gig, all these people from town came out to see the Radiators and it was our big day — like, these people were coming out and here's our chance to impress them. But when we played, there was much spitting and jeering and a fight sort of broke out and some of the Prunes had to, you know, take the guys out.

"And it was only because we were young. I mean, you put these young boys up on stage and they're playing their music — and you're twenty-one. I mean, why should you dance to them? Isn't there a bit of an ego thing involved? Of course there was. Let's face it, most of these people would like to be involved in music — so they get a bit annoyed at these young whippersnappers up there: "they're doing it and I'm not".

"Adam was looking after the money and when they'd see Adam, they'd think "oh, they're all rich, they don't need the money". Which wasn't the case at all — we were all smashed, especially Adam because his parents were not at all into him playing music. He got no financial help at all. He worked very hard for anything he ever got!" (loud cheering and clapping).

"Adam had the right attitude when he got involved with the band — he said, "this is it, this is what I want to do" and he just forgot about his schoolwork and all that, much to his parents' distress. And I must admit it was his determination which spread to the band and eventually

my schoolwork started to deterioriate. And Larry's!"

INTO THE DEEP END — THE HOW, WHY AND WHAT OF THE SONGS

Bono: "I never write lyrics until the last minute because they're constantly building as we work out the song. They build subconsciously because I found that I can write exactly what I *want* to write subconsciously, better than anything sitting down and trying. When the song is complete — when the idea is right — I then assemble the lyrics.

"They all point to one thing — getting people to think for themselves. There's also a reaction against heavy advertising and television images and things like that. I remember seeing heroes on television — people like James Bond and so on — and thinking, 'I'm not very good looking — I'm not going to get things like that' and being unhappy about it. Also the constant pushing of perfection — beautiful boys and beautiful girls. Intelligence in school — *everything that it seemed you were not* — was pushed at you and I had a bit of a reaction against that. I personally had a very heavy adolescence — emotional turmoil, that sort of thing. We feel that we're qualified to comment on things like that because we are teenagers.

"Everybody has a spiritual awareness — but in rock music it tends to be forgotten. Teenagers think about questions like — it there a God? Or refusing to go to service — why? It's just finding out what you want in life or what you are in life — and the spiritual element is there.

""Out of Control" is about waking up on your eighteenth birthday and realising that you're 18 years old and that the two most important decisions in your life have nothing to do with you — being born and dying. The song is from the child's point of view and it's about a vicious circle. He becomes a delinquent but the psychologist says "it's in his childhood". No matter what he does — it can't be because he wants to, it's always because of what went before and there's no decision in anything. Then again, that's slightly spiritual — the question what is happening if you've no freedom?

"The lyrics change on stage. That's something that fascinates me about Iggy Pop. I knew he constructed lyrics in his head and never wrote them down. When I saw him on stage, I could see the way he changed them. You're just finding out what you really want to say as opposed to what is correct grammatically. I like the sound of words, as well — like in "The Fool" some of the lyrics don't make sense but they're there for the sound of the words. Like: *"Alive in an ocean a world of glad ice"* ... that sentence came because of its actual colour.

"We're serious about ... like, everyone has emotions and we're serious about them. They come out in our lyrics and our attitude but it's not all intended to be serious," Dave: "We're trying to avoid being shallow and one-dimensional.

"It's like the difference between the comic and the hard-covered book."

Bono: "But fun is part of it — we're trying to capture all emotions." Larry; "Like, "Cartoon World"."

Dave: "It's comic strip. We might lack a bit of humour but we have enough humour in ourselves. I think that'll develop in the music. We're aware that we're not going to change the world or anything. But if we can reach *some* of the people".

IMAGES, AUDIENCES AND THE END

Bono: "There's two types of character being portrayed on stage: the Child — or the Boy — and the Fool, the clown. These are the two sides of what we want to project. If we always come across as serious, then we're not succeeding.

"We have no intention of playing the hero. We are *acting out* the role of hero. Off-stage I would consider myself a very Joe Bloggs-type of person. But the movement on stage is integral. You're trying to point people towards the stage. You're saying "Look at me". It's very silly (laughs) — you're jumping up and down, saying "look at me". Very much like a child.

"Sometimes there is a danger of me being a bit patronising — I don't really mean to. This night there was a girl in the audience and I said "what's your name?" and she got all coy. But the other friend *knew* what to say. She just moved in front of the microphone and shouted: "FUCK OFF YOU BLOCKHEAD! I knew I couldn't compete, so I just walked away, holding my head down in embarrassment. I was the prick!

"We hope for a type of cross-over audience. Like the name U-2 was chosen because of its ambiguity, if you like — because it wasn't attached to any trend be it old wave or new wave. We want to stand up on our own.

"We're also determined to achieve a position where we have artistic freedom and where we can affect people the way we want to affect them. We want to get that position, that artistic freedom, which derives from money and success and we'll work very hard to get there. And we're willing to compromise to a certain extent — but the music is very believed in ...

Adam: "It's a quest for perfection, as we see it. In the next two years, we're going to develop so much more — it's going to be a continuing, growing and maturing process".

They speak well for themselves, U-2. ∎

Niall Stokes.
Vol 3 No. 9 October 26 1979

Adam Clayton: Pic Bernard Farrell.

24

U2 Sign to Island

1980. Early Island publicity photo by Sheila Rock.

The story of U2's international recording contract , March 1980.

U-2 have signed a major international recording contract with the Island label, it was confirmed on Monday.

The contract which had been anticipated locally for some time, will entail the release of four albums over its four year duration – after which Island have the usual options – and in the first 12 months, U2 will issue no less than three singles and their debut album, the latter to be recorded in August for an October release date. It's expected that only one of these singles will also be available on the album.

The Island deal is a world-wide one, binding for all territories except Ireland, while in the U.S, U-2 material will be issued on the Warners label.

U-2, who already have two locally released CBS singles to their credit, will be recording their first Island 45 – the song as yet undecided – over the Easter weekend in Dublin's Windmill Studios. Set to produce the record is Martin "Zero" Hannett, whose association with the Factory label, has seen him work with Joy Division, as well as producing records for John Cooper-Clarke, The Teardrop Explodes and others. Hannett was chosen at the suggestion of U-2 themselves, who were reportedly very impressed with the production on Joy Division's "Unknown Pleasures" album.

U-2 will be handled by Ian Flooks' Wasted Talent agency (formerly Derek Block) who are also responsible for the Clash and the Police amongst others.

Live plans include a major British tour to coincide with their debut single release in May, followed by Summer dates – including outdoor concerts – in Europe. Once those commitments are fulfilled the band will be returning home for an Irish tour.

Having secured what is undoubtedly the most important international recording contract for a local band since the Rats signed for Ensign, U-2 were understandably reported to be "ecstatic", looking on the deal as a vindication that "sooner or later you get the deal you need". The band, who swept to victory in this year's Hot Press readers' poll, also expressed a debt of gratitude to Bill Graham of this parish, who was not only the first media person to champion the band but who also played a small but hardly insignificant role by introducing them to their manager Paul McGuinness. ∎

Vol. 3. No. 20 March 29th 1980

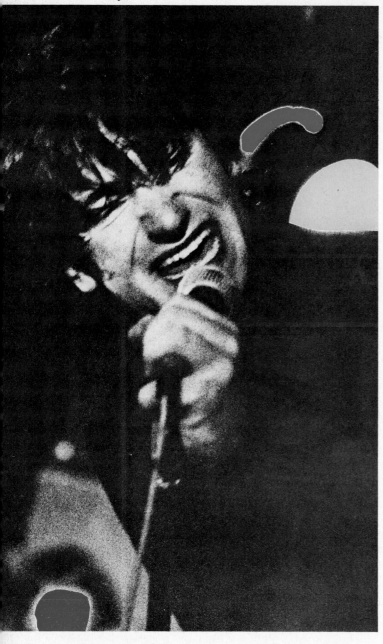

Live Bono, Pic: Colm Henry.

Close to the Edge

Peter Owens sees U2 in The Half Moon, London.

AT THE appointed time, U-2 commandeered the shoebox stage and set to the task of expanding it with the determination of an SAS squad. Within moments they had stretched it to gargantuan proportions, the Edge doggedly elbowing himself an action space, Bono straining and reaching out and up and Adam cowing the impressive bulk of the p.a. beside him into an easy submission. The last date of the first full tour and it seemed like a homecoming, although most of the audience still didn't know them from Adam – well, from Cain anyway.

There's something frightening about pure joy, a tiny fear that if you succumb totally to it you'll never return, and Bono inculcates that vital tension — the wariness that the thin line between ecstasy and epilepsy might at any moment snap — with natural ease.

It won't, of course, because Bono has the rare gift of captivation without putting himself in danger. He surges, he clutches at anything within reach, the mike stand, the p.a., the lighting frame. The Edge just becomes more and more quietly inscrutable, the hint of a smile fleetingly visible, and Adam lolls and sprawls into a disjointed vision of straw hair.

"Tick Tock" both opens and closes, and again the live version is structured differently from the record, Bono's one-man chapel choir rushing in straight after the first verse, an angel where fools fear to tread. And when it's finished, there's another 200 U-2 fans to be added to the list. No further calling cards needed, the battle is already won and the rest of the set is in a sense, unnecessary. But for 40 more minutes they anchor down the goodwill without respite, lambasting the crowd into surrender.

And for the first time, the inclusion of all "U-2 – 3" in succession is not noticeable, the graft into newer material invisible because of the maturer, more fully realised arrangements. Sting is somewhere in there now in "Out of Control", but that's no slight as Bono's voice now occasionally develops a more corrosive edge with use. Larry, for me once the slight chink in the armour, has pulled through with honours and is now a far more positive force, pushing where once he held back.

U-2 are like an imminent thunderstorm, inducing an electrostatic breathlessness, the prickling of the skin, the uncomfortable gnawing on the soles of the feet. The difference between them and almost any other band is that such effect, the key to satisfaction, is normally achieved either by the bluster of the best metal or the aloofness of "modernists". U-2 achieve it all simply by smiling. Very shortly Britain will be thanking them for it.■

Peter Owens
Vol. 4 No. 2 June 20th 1980

Larry

Pic: Colm Henry.

The Battle of Britain

U2 prepare to depart Dun Laoghaire. Pic: Colm Henry.

Bill Graham joins U2 on a major British assault.

Twilight, another time another place, where emotions will touch, collide, jostle and electrify into tantalizing shapes. Into the twilight zone where this temporary lodger strives to maintain detachment. Into a twilight zone between two countries and two cultures go U-2. Into this twilight zone and you realise how mistaken it is to measure magic. It's the endlessly replayed battle between print and music. And can Bono's ideal child read?

Recollected in tranquillity are three totally dissimilar nights wherein U-2 were disturbed, then contented and finally erupted.

You get scared and exhilarated, worried and enthralled and then so protective of the U-2 child. You know he's long past the walking stage, you know he's restless and impatient to cavort and provoke. You know he wishes to will miracles, to change darkness into light. And you get unnerved and foresee the grey forces that abound and bide their time.

Stunned, you simultaneously admire and are alarmed by U-2's ambition. Some bands have a tryst with rock 'n' roll destiny and U-2 could conceivably be one of those. Robert Fripp speaks of rock 'n' roll being the encounter between innocence and history. Unadorned, undistracted, U-2's themes are precisely that.

Let's take the boat to England.

We've arrived and to what? Mucho publicity courtesy of *Sounds* and a photo and accompanying paragraph in *Time Out* — a prestigious and encouraging recognition. This is essential because U-2's current game is "find the audience". They've played London before and built up the first traces of a following but amid the competing tribes of the Capital, they've got to mark out, advertise and populate their own parish. None among us doubt the band's capacity to win over any audience that arrives with open-hearted curiosity — rather it's getting them to appear that's crucial.

And the following Thursday night at the Clarendon in Hammersmith, the gameplan appears to go awry.

29

The Edge in pensive mood. Pic: Colm Henry.

Afterwards we commiserate and realise that the date has not been publicised by *Time Out* and that Thursday is the low day before the weekend — but there's a discouraging and unbalanced turn-out.

The Clarendon is a first floor hall in a hotel of Victorian vintage. It requires about 500 to pack it but only 200 arrive and that includes a high guest list quota of interested bands and Island Records staff. I wander around looking for teenagers — they're hard to find.

And the circumstances of environment and audience make for a struggling, emotionally naked gig. There's nothing inaccurate or unfeeling about the band's playing but the confrontation between band and the worldiest audience of the tour has its moments when the dare-devil comes close to desperation. With wild determination, Bono keeps bringing his toys to them, keeps demanding 'Look at this' but the chemistry is odd and you know he knows it. The audience has come to measure U-2 against their building reputation as 'at least this week's thing' and won't be willed into enjoyment. And at moments I'm wondering if some aren't inwardly tut-tutting at Bono for lowering his front and making a disgracefully unreserved exhibition of himself. He reveals himself to the core, he shows his want; that isn't playing the game according to the rules of that modern spectator sport called rock 'n' roll. It's madness, another category entirely.

I feel small clouds of bemusement in the atmosphere and partially understand *Sounds* journalist Dave McCullough's anger at a similar date at the Nashville where under-20's weren't permitted — the empathy necessary for shared euphoria is absent. Despite a small crowd bopping around the front, Bono just can't feel the audience. Each number gains applause, but it isn't enough, it isn't enough.

The lack is answered. Suddenly out of the unsettled climate wafts a moment of sublime dignity. A sequence of guitar chords — the linking passage between two new songs "An Cat Dubh" and "The Heart of a Child" — stealthily spirals upwards and for once the echoing acoustics assist. Soothing, a peace offering, this vision of unwasted youth, that sounds like 'Albatross' as reinterpreted by Eno, transforms the mood and when the song is over there's a muted sighing cheer of recognition. Such sweet thunder!

Doubt diminishes, though Bono's still fraught on the encore "I Will Follow" and a triplet of fans joins them on stage. One wears a tee-shirt of Sid Vicious, the man whose manipulated inauthentic self-detonating rebellion represents all U-2 stand against. A small stubborn step forward for U-2 has been achieved.

"It was tense, it was wrought iron, it was big because of the volume and the echo" Bono reflects. "It was vast.

It was most peculiar. The audience were tense because I think they were in a place they weren't used to being in. It was cold – it was a peculiar place upstairs in a hotel, a large dance-floor with light-shades, at the same time bare. It was the unknown and the unknown is always very interesting. Last night was more of emotion, of the band relaxing into the audience and into the music".

Bono can be the band's best reviewer. The first two dates are a complete contrast. At the Half Moon Club in Herne Hill, south of the Thames, a warm and comfortable pub where the dressing-room is the manager's living room, U-2 gain a full house and Paul McGuinness smilingly ambles across to inform me that this is a landmark night, the first time U-2 have sold out an English venue.

It shows in the music also. U-2 play a much more contented, less abrasive set, their ardour somewhat cushioned in this cosy pub. I like the set, I smile more than the previous night but it's not an environment to bring out the performing extremes of Kid Galahad and his companions – even though for the encore Bono leaps off stage to serenade the audience from the raised enclosure where the mixing desk and us flunkies are located. It's a good gig, well done boys and all that, an opportunely-timed confidence-builder for the remaining two dates at the Moonlight Club and then at the Marquee, supporting the Photos.

About this point it's customary to relate the on-the-road antics and anecdotes of the band in question. With U-2 however, one isn't dealing with a band whose alcoholically and/or otherwise induced acts of privileged delinquency keep their publicists merrily feeding the gossip columns with froth. With the exception of Adam Clayton, who twice escorts manager Paul McGuinness in pursuit of nocturnal revelry, U-2 aren't tempted by the bright lights. For a rock band they are early risers and early sleepers – U-2's cautious rationing of distractions is further evidence of their dedication and the manner in which their energy is channelled so concentratedly into their music.

We're also unlucky on the two nights we do venture out. After Herne Hill we drive to the Belgravia Carnival only to discover we've been misinformed. It finished the previous night. Then there was the great Lookalikes party mystery.

Friday, tour manager Jim Nicholson meets their drummer Mike Mesbur and elicits the information that the Lookalikes will be holding a party Saturday night in their Wandsworth house. So at the appointed time off drives the whole party, to discover a totally darkened and vacated house. Tails between the tyres of our Mercedes van, we return to the Earls Court apartment the band have rented for the duration and ring around to learn that the list of social victims extends to the

> **At the Half Moon Club, U2 gain a full house and Paul McGuinness smilingly ambles across to inform me that this is a landmark night, the first time U2 have sold out at an English venue.**

Tearjerkers, Moondogs and the Lookalikes publisher. Someone excuses the Lookalikes by suggesting they've probably overshot on their day's recording session but as the unofficially nominated shop-steward for the disappointed, I can say that only a fully signed and witnessed statement will be accepted in explanation.

So all I can tell you and Dr. Conor Cruise O'Brien on his Thames house-boat is that Bono talks to *The Observer* in his underpants.

Saturday morning in the common room of the flat, everyone's making or eating their breakfast and immune to the chatter around him, there's Bono in his white y-fronts, nattering away on the phone to Robin Denselow, writer of the "Upfront" rock snippets in the Sunday's colour supplement. Readers of a sensitive disposition can rest assured that both he and the rest of the band were fully clothed for the *Hot Press* interview which follows next.

In that school we were allowed a freedom to think about things because we got to know about things like girls and how they interacted with boys at an early age. So that didn't become a hang-up.

"Obviously smoking wasn't encouraged but at the same time – and I can only see it now – it was not so authoritarian to make us feel, right we're going out to smoke, we're going down the pub at lunchtime to get drunk against these people, these oppressive faces – because they weren't oppressive, so what was the point?"

U-2's chemistry deriving from their beginnings as a school band may be their secret ingredient but the receptacle for that chemistry, Mount Temple Comprehensive appears to have been a very special school. As Ireland's first comprehensive, its pupils suffered none of the totalitarian emotional suffocation which has disfigured so much of Irish education. Nor were they conscripted into a religious system of no joy; U-2 come scarless from their school.

"Adam really knows the two sides of the coin because he was also in another style of school" advises the Edge and Adam who went to prep school and then as a boarder to St. Columba's till he was 16 confirms the difference of experiences.

"To be perfectly honest I rebelled against the privileged society (in St. Columba's) even though I was part of it, which is totally hypocritical, I suppose. But I just thought there were a lot of people who weren't really very important human beings. They were just living on something else, the fact they were part of that society was what gave them importance. And I don't think it worked."

Refer to Bob Geldof and his embittering experiences in Blackrock College, refer coincidentally in this issue to Joey Barry of the Spies and his comments about the Christian Brothers and marvel at U-2's fortune. They haven't had to waste energy in emotion-consuming and distorting campaigns against Church and teacher. They hadn't to suffer the confusion induced by a system that claims to teach people to be saints but in reality compels and trains them to be rebels. It also explains the odd angle from which U-2 approach rock and its notions of rebellion.

"That's half the thrill of teenage drinking," says Bono "I can remember drinking because it was an exciting thing to do at an early age. It was something you weren't supposed to do. At the same time I got very bored very quickly with it, whereas many of my counterparts in other schools around Dublin didn't.

"No, I'm not from the same privileged background as Adam. He lived in Malahide whereas I lived in Ballymun and the people around me didn't get so bored with it so easy. I questioned even things like smoking. Obviously I used to smoke paper or whatever it was. But I got bored very quickly with those terms of rebellion because, unlike my neighbours, I wasn't being told all the time not to do this.

"I wouldn't question anybody's leisure time if there's been a decision behind it. But I'm afraid where I've come from, there's a very definite thing which is drinking tonight, drinking tomorrow night, drinking Thursday night, drinking Friday night. That is the trend of people at 18.

"Why? Because they've nowhere to go. Why? Because they can't really think of anything else to do. Why? Maybe because things are apathetic now, so other forms of leisure — even football — are declining. That is a pattern they're falling into and they're not so much thinking about it as wandering there, being headed there. And it's a safe thing."

And he continues by criticising the double standards of Governments that promote Health Education campaigns against drink and nicotine whilst simultaneously raking in vast revenues from the habit.

Matters of attitude, the means to avoid contamination of the spirit and will — these are the points Bono is arguing, though he is careful not be perceived as a crusading misanthropic puritan. He adds: "I'm not anti-drink ... all of us drink occasionally. But I don't think we're involved in what I call rock 'n' roll masturbation, which is that you're in a band, you get wrecked with other members of other bands and it gets in the papers and everybody laughs Ho ho ho."

It was this exact refusal to participate in the rock 'n' roll swindle and to be manoeuvred into a sub-culture of gratuitous wasteful squabbling and easily-policed and controlled rebellion that made U-2 controversial through '78 and '79. They weren't to be re-routed by the tyranny of fashion. Although it must be stated that U-2 were lucky. It isn't every individual who finds, as these four did, the right chemistry of friends, allies and circumstances.

Nonetheless Bono's point about their differences with other factions in Dublin remains: "We are anti-laziness, we are anti-apathy with no direction. I am really glad to see that some people with whom we've had previous disagreements are actually doing something positive themselves. I've no time for cynicism with no direction. I've no time for people who complain and sit around looking into space. There's a guy in Dublin who we all know, Brummie, who's at least trying to arrange concerts. Whatever. I still can't relate to the guy himself but I like that — that I can appreciate. But I've no time for people who are casual rebels. They remind me of the hippies of the past who would get stoned and sink into the day."

The Edge enters with his contribution, the guitarist talking about the 'pregnant' Irish author: "It's a term I've heard in literary circles and because he's always in the middle of his novel he can always slag off everybody else's. And you know he'll always be in that position telling everybody what they're doing wrong."

Bono contrasts such attitudes with their own. "A lot of people knocked U-2 at the start because we were young and wide-eyed and they weren't doing anything themselves. At least U-2 realised we had problems. We realised we were wide-eyed, we realised we had problems. We realised we must find people who *did* know and find out and we worked hard and that's the point."

And Adam tells of his incredulity about a ridiculous discussion with another Dublin band: "I was shocked because they were advocating that the only way to get on in Dublin, or the music business anywhere, was by crapping on people."

Saving that band's embarrassment by naming them, his story concerns an incident wherein said outfit played petty power games to headline. Adam was arguing that "Goodwill among Dublin bands had been sacrificed" by

Bono: (inset Larry, Edge and Paul McGuinness) Pic: Colm Henry

Larry

Pic: Aaran Rappaport/Sipa Press

Adam

Pic: Aaron Rappaport/Sipa Press

Larry: the drummer who came in from the cold. Pic: Colm Henry.

their methods but he was met by the counter-assertion that it was a victory, the band had headlined and "it was more important than the goodwill of people": "And I said if you're thinking like that, it's no wonder you're still in the position you are, in Dublin. Because I think that's terrible and it's even worse to admit it."

Bono takes up the theme. "Maybe it was sent down from the Rats, that to get on you get your own way, you have a direction and you fight to get there. But we were never like that. We realised that as a self-sufficient unit, we couldn't break through. Let's accumulate knowledge, let's talk to people in the different areas and find out. And we found out knowledge, we discovered knowledge. We went to the right people at the right

time. We got the right manager and that's always been the way. And in music we always put in the same effort."

But not everybody was sympathetically responding.

There was a crisis point when U-2 almost crashed to earth, when the bravado of their idealistic plans met the music industry in recession and cynical turmoil. For the six months before U-2 finally came to reside with Island, the organisation was under severe financial pressure.

As manager, Paul McGuinness' assets have included not only his ability and prior experience but also his lucrative career as a director of advertising films, a

36

factor which both allowed him to invest money in U-2 beyond their contemporaries and to approach his bank manager with more self-confidence than other Irish band managers when circumstances required.

But when, last Autumn, U-2 planned their first venture to England, they were shook by their first taste of short-sighted London Machiavellianism. Their dates were meant to be financed by the advance of a publishing deal but the company involved, at the last and most pressurising moment, halved the advance in the hope of swinging a cheaper deal. McGuinness put down the phone and in 48 hours he and the band made up the shortfall, by borrowing £3,000 from friends and family.

A blow parried — but at the start of the year it was followed by the EMI debacle. Negotiations had already fallen through with both CBS and A & M but EMI, through the advocacy of their A & R man, Tom Nolan, were taking a much more serious interest. Two other EMI executives travelled with Nolan to Dublin whereupon the party sat down at the back of the Baggot Inn — and then departed to watch the Specials on the Old Grey Whistle Test!

The ironies of the incident were black and morale-shattering. EMI, who despite Nolan's insistence had already passed on the Specials, sacked him and U-2 retired to recover.

"We were demoralised and we were broke. What should we do then? Lie in our own self-pity?" Bono asks rhetorically.

"No." he answers himself." We decided what we were going to do. We were going to play a headline concert tour around Ireland and we were going to headline at the Stadium and that was our way of fighting against the pressures, to go in exactly the opposite way and to show people we were full of confidence."

And it was at the Stadium that Bill Stewart of Island arrived and according to Bono 'offered us a deal on the spot': "Which, and this should be noted, we complained about. We still knew what we wanted and we disagreed with this, this and this. They could have said 'like it or lump it, we're going'. And if they had left, where were we? But we believed, because we weren't going to be second, we weren't going to drop our aim. And in fact they have honoured that."

But the soul of the band must be finally located in its music. The same application and dedication informs their working methods. At this point U-2 could justifiably relax but each available weekday in Dublin they trek out to their Malahide rehearsal room to continue their course of musical self-improvement.

This results in U2 possessing an intimidating number of songs — over forty by their estimate — as the time nears, to decide on material to record for their debut album this August. And such prolific creation also means a set that is in a state of constant flux — so here in London, besides the affecting "An Cat Dubh/Heart Of A Child" pairing, U-2 are also debuting "Saturday Night" and "I Will Follow".

The Edge likens their work methods to that of a sculptor in his studio "We get a block or if you like three pieces of rock and you've just got to chisel away with them and get them into shape."

Larry Mullen who's been sitting quietly so far explains a key change in his role: "Adam and Dave and Bono used to write songs and say Larry you come down at four and we'll put drums to it. And in fact in a review of Peter Owens, he said I saw U-2 before and I thought the drums were the weak link. And that was very true because Dave, Adam and Bono were writing songs and I was coming down to put the drums on and I wasn't seeing how the songs were being made. So now myself and Adam are writing songs together so the bass and drums are working in a way they weren't before."

One detail, one anecdote, one teacher left — Mannix Flynn. This person remembers wandering through Stephens Green one Sunday lunchtime to find Bono and Gavin of the Prunes with their drama tutor. Bono flares with affection when I mention Mannix.

"Mannix Flynn is a guy I respect. I just love him, his whole thing. He's Dublin to me — he's great. He's evolved from a very rough part of town. He has no cynicism — like he wouldn't resent Adam because Adam lives in Malahide. He's quite open on all areas and he treats people like people. He has a lot of knowledge about the 'space', which is what he calls the stage. And how to be on that stage and how your body is on that stage and how to talk to people with your body. And we studied mime with him and with people that he knows."

Adam concurs about the importance of Mannix, the former Project actor, collaborator in "The Liberty Suit",

> **"We discovered knowledge. We went to the right people at the right time. We got the right manager. That's always been the way and in music we put in the same effort." — *Bono***

ex-borstal inmate and occasional shop steward of Grafton St. "I think in terms of somebody to talk to, he was crucial because just his ideas and perspective on life are really important."

Bono adds, "That was an important area for us. That's why we studied the mime — to loosen us up, to try and

Adam by the sea. Pic: Colm Henry.

perform on stage and we're only at the beginning of that ..."

As London finds.

It was a rising at the Moonlight. A superlative extraordinary affair that prompted Paul McGuinness to honour it by buying the band a bottle of champagne, a rare ritual, reserved for very special performances. The 'Find The Audience' game was over, the house was packed — forty minutes before U-2 took the stage — Adam having to embarrassedly placate the latecoming group of fans who've arrived from Herne Hill. U-2 just raped, pillaged and plundered the Moonlight.

It was Bono's instinct again. I don't believe his associates ever wavered from the same level throughout the three dates — if anything they made more mistakes tonight than during the other two — but the theme of this tour is how Bono reacted with such intuitive accuracy to each environment.

He just conducts and re-generates the mood and tonight any anxiety or temptation to relax is passed. Every ploy in the book, including the Iggy swan-dive into the audience, works. He just energises through to that well-nigh fanatical power of rock, where you don't know whether to savour, be exalted or frightened now that the beast is roaming the hall.

You just feel a rare power and intensity, one that doesn't hide itself or role-play within accepted styles. You feel exhilaration, obvious pride and shudder because unlike 99.99% of the company, you know this is only the beginning. In Ireland, U-2 and Bono have existed in a well-protected enclave; they can't look back now.

Such is the emotion — the details are secondary. You saw Larry open-mouthed like never before, you felt a band and a performer whose existential grasp of the drama of rock could push this entertainment into shapes not previously premeditated.

You got careful, you got too fearful, too protective, to rave. You note an intensity, a desire for communion that extends far beyond matey, laddish revelry or anguished mutual therapy. A force unleashed, a force controlled, a dynamo in search of a destiny.

And a destiny in search of a new dynamo! Afterwards in the flat I ask Adam about the dressing-room comments. What did the fans say? What was their line? He says they were wary, they thought we'd be superstars.

Even the fans get scared and exhilarated, worried and enthralled — and then so protective of the U-2 child! ■

They'll survive.

Bill Graham
Vol 4 No. 4
July 19th, 1980

Bono looks up while Adam remains in light.
Pic: Eamonn O'Dwyer.

The Boy Can't Help It

Declan Lynch reviews the debut album "Boy".

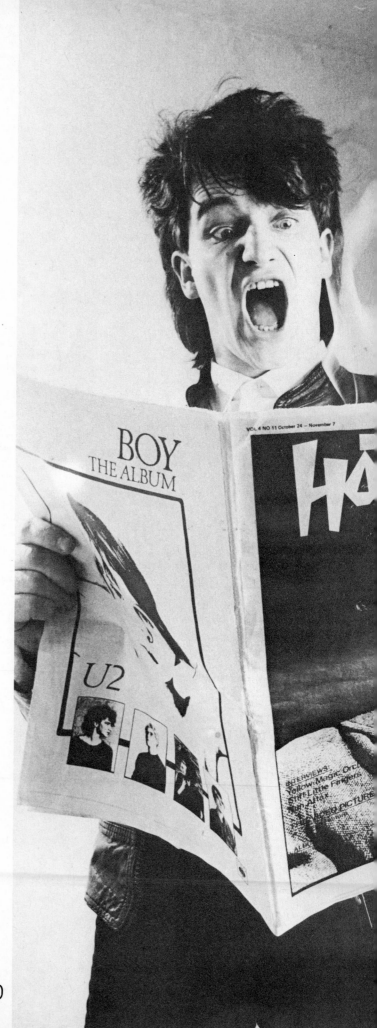

"U-2 MAKE me think", it's been said. That criterion is used a lot these days because as rock 'n' roll gets older, its priorities and values change. It spreads itself out and becomes more adjustable, like a toy.

It couldn't really be said of Gene Vincent or Jerry Lee Lewis that they make you *think*. They hardly even had to stand at the cross roads and decide which road to take, because through natural innocence and naivete, they were relieved of that burden. They made you *know*.

Now it seems like we've come such a long way without really going anywhere at all. U-2 seem anxious to draw the brakes, so they mention 'innocence' and they use the word 'spiritual' a great deal. (Come, come boys, let's be reasonable, you're not selling us *that* old dummy, *surely*?) (Bono is nodding his head, I think he means it.)

Easier said than done of course, factors such as background, education, time, and place being the salient ones. The days of liberation through primitivism are gone, and the psychological dance goes round and round, the dancers think, the thinkers dance.

We're walking a kind of plank. The record shows that rock 'n' roll went sour when it became a vehicle for 'self-awareness', and when people started seeing God in guitar solos. There's a different kind of hippy dippyism on the prowl at the moment, with groups wallowing in their own so-abject misery, even bragging about it.

U-2 could beat the snare. Their music is so positive, so optimistic, it can make you think straight. As distinct from the Rolling Stones, who took the Devil's music and dressed it up in white man's clothes, and white man's drugs, and whose fans *knew* that the Stones *knew* what

I read the news today. Oh Boy.

they were up to, U-2's aim is to forget everything they ever knew and start all over again. (Impossible!).

Certainly in terms of the great, glorious tradition of Irish rock, they stand out. Lynott was at times capable of honesty, but mostly hid his inadequacy behind the myth of Lizzy. He played along with everything, he was cute, he kept the wrong company and at heart he was the Darling of Dingwalls.

Geldof's road to freedom was through his ego, and while we all *knew* it was a front and that behind the mask there lay a wonderful, cuddly human, we decided that a joke is just a joke.

In comparison, U-2 have so far led a sheltered musical life, and the milder rock climate that has been apparent of late, has allowed them to grow naturally. They are not at all warped by the myths of rock 'n' roll and in terms of male involvement with rock, they are idealistic and less prone to the hedonistic practices of others. I think they stand for something, and I think that's important.

This album echoes with sounds and sentiments which are unfamiliar. There is a romanticism there, a dream-like quality, which is offset by a new aggression, a new directness. No one track is radically different to another in construction or in texture. This is an explosion of the emerging sound of U-2; the cards are now on the table, and the only direction to take is straight ahead.

For their already large fan club, "Boy" will be practically a restrospective album. "Out of Control", "Twilight" and "Stories For Boys" have been re-recorded, "A Day Without Me" is here also. "Shadows In Tall Trees" and "Another Time, Another Place" have been taken out of mothballs.

Nevertheless, I find it almost impossible to react negatively to U-2's music. It rushes your senses, it's so sharp; every song seems like it's been lying under the tree all year, and at Christmas it's taken out of its box and shown to everybody, open-mouthed.

I wouldn't worry about U-2 selling out because I know they will. "Out", after all, is the only way to sell and once you show an interest in the shifting of units, there's no point feeling guilty about the extent. It will be interesting to see if they cope better than others, but as regards railing against the music business, I've lost interest.

For now, U-2 are full of bluster, almost keeling over with the weight of energy on board. They have given birth to their own kind of cool, and they are as important or as trivial as you want to make them.

Make them sweat. ∎

Declan Lynch
Vol. 4 No. 10
October 10th, 1980

Adam

Pic: Colm Henry.

Larry

Pic: Anton Corbijn.

Growing Up in Public

Neil McCormick, a school friend of the band, looks back and looks forward with U2.

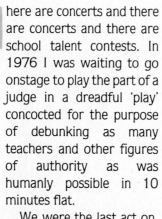

There are concerts and there are concerts and there are school talent contests. In 1976 I was waiting to go onstage to play the part of a judge in a dreadful 'play' concocted for the purpose of debunking as many teachers and other figures of authority as was humanly possible in 10 minutes flat.

We were the last act on, following a group called Feedback, consisting of four school-friends: Larry Mullen, David Evans, Paul Hewson and Adam Clayton. But as the group opened up with a version of Peter Frampton's "Show Me The Way", I knew there was nothing that would make me follow them onstage. I was awe-struck. I was frightened. They were probably terrible but it was my first live electric-music and it was love at first sight.

In there somewhere was the start of the path that would lead me to where I am now (sitting up at a ridiculous hour of the night trying to finish this article before I am consumed by onrushing deadlines and editorial wrath). And in there somewhere was the start of the path that would lead U-2 to where they are now (Adam painting London town red, Larry, the Edge (Dave) and Bono (Paul) sitting around their bedroom in various states of undress trying to explain what happened on that day).

Me: "I was very impressed. I'd never seen a live group before" ... Bono: "I'd never seen a live group before". Me: "I was knocked out". Bono: "I was knocked out. There was, from the very start, the evidence I believe of a spark. We walked up on that stage, I was playing guitar, and when I heard that D-Chord, I got some kick. When

U2 in 1980. Pic: Colm Henry

I heard that D-chord it was like starting up a motorbike. There was something special there.

"And the audience went *wild*! And I think we might as well forget the actual piece 'cause that wasn't important" ... (much laughter) "but, it was the first thing I ever sang well. That was a very special concert, that was one of the best concerts of our lives. That's in the top-five concerts to this day. And we built ourselves around that spark. I'll tell you, it was like four blind kids blustering away, and there was the evidence of just a little light in the corner and we started to work towards that. Getting to grips with our instruments, getting to grips with performance. And the light was getting clearer. Right now it's like standing in the daylight as far as I'm concerned. Looking around me I've grown up. I mean you're talking about when we formed, you're talking about 15 year olds."

U-2 have travelled, grown, expanded and exploded in four years. The speed of life pulsing through their veins, they exhilarate us with their own excitement. Their sound is nothing new, just some bass, drums, guitar and singing, but it is everything new — expansive and

expressive, and emotional. A unique group in any terms, not just Irish, they took the forward path, through hard work, speedily becoming Ireland's most respected, fresh, admired rock 'n' roll sons and lovers. They transferred their excitement to places across the water with remarkable ease, and as they released a testament to their strength called "Boy", we stood back with baited breath to see what would happen next.

And we will see, we will see.

All this time U-2 have constantly changed and evolved. A single-minded pursuit of ideals has taken them from sloppy cover versions to sloppy originals to tight originals to different originals. Their sound has been shaped and pushed and stamped U-2, but they don't *stop* there. Their lyrics are beginning to come together with the music. And live they are honest and open (to ridicule often): they communicate, they shake. And hey Mama, we're all shakin' now!

As they struggled from one point to another I was around to cheer them on and see what I could get out of it — not blind to their faults I hope, but aware of their strength and potential. Last July in a 'suprise' visit to the Project, they proved beyond a shadow of a doubt that

any faith has been well-placed. That one short gig did something to me that allows me to believe in rock 'n' roll music despite all of its detractors, rock 'n' roll as the essence of youthful emotional communication: all the power of sensurround, the vision of cinemascope, the colour of technicolour, the essential bridging appeal of honesty and care. Hello, Hello (Stories for boys, girls and anyone else who wants to join in).

The scene is set for a startling denouement. Someone told me recently that at least three members of U-2 were very committed Christians. Crash, I came tumbling down. I am an agnostic, and so, to a large extent is rock 'n' roll, celebrating material rather than spiritual saviours (sex, drugs, drink, maaan!). Christianity's relationship with rock 'n' roll is a less than favourable one — in search of answers, rock has constantly looked to mysticism, or non-western religions. Christianity has always been the predominant Western system of beliefs, but its values are not the values of rock music — its more celebrated musical practitioners (Cliff Richard, After The Fire) prove why the devil should have all the good music. Brandishing nothing but a wimpy understanding of the essential imagination, directness and aggressive edge that provides rock with its power, they fail to face up to, enhance or explain the problems of this or any other life.

Think of a generation's gasp of disappointment as Dylan, a beacon to many in the search for answers, took up the banner of Christianity. That way is too crusading, too safe and too easy.

Or is it? Rewind. Rethink. Re-adjust my own prejudices. When I heard about U-2 I was, for a short while, bitterly disappointed, I wanted to shout at them, but they were friends, people I admired and respected, so I thought about it and when we met to talk, I didn't shout at them. (Maybe I will next time).

It's a touch and go situation here. A delicate line — there is a lot I want to say, a lot of dots that need to be joined, but there is a lot that U-2 don't want to talk about, a lot that they said which they asked me not to print, so let's touch and go.

Bono: "It's very important that ... we don't want to be the band that talks about God. I do not want to talk about it in terms of music — anything that has to be said on that personal level is in the music or on stage and I don't want to go through the media. I don't want to talk to the world about it because we will face a situation where people will see us with a banner over our heads. That is not the way U-2 is gonna work. If there is anything in what we have to say, it will be seen in our lives, in our music and in our performance."

So let's talk about albums and gigs and rock stars in their underpants ... but it's no use. You want to know, and I want to know, and we both want to understand.

Whether your beliefs are Christian or not, it is important to anyone interested, anyone who cares about U-2 to understand better what they are, who they are and why they are.

You know U-2 are a very special group. I noticed too, a long time ago. They have not always been Christians but they have always been special. So let's have some history and some talk and join those dots I mentioned earlier.

U-2 have an original sound because they approached it in an honest and natural way. An original way. They faced their flaws and worked from the most basic blueprint available — who they were and what they could do. The dependence on 'sub-conscious' development, something that is also found in their songwriting where Bono shapes most of his lyrics onstage, allows things to flow through in a natural way. But this approach is tempered by an intelligent awareness of what they *want* to do ...

Edge: "We knew what sort of material we wanted — so, if you want a particular idea, right, you start picking instruments and amps and effects and what have you. When you start doing that, you start to develop a sound. Then when you *have* a sound, you find certain things work better on that and you get it to a certain vocabulary of music. And before you know what's happening you're on your way to style, a sound and musicianship."

Bono: "We haven't stepped out very far to the right or to the left. The changes are subtle. Originality should depend on individuality rather than the obvious claims to being different. Like people using spoons instead of guitars. That's the easy way out. That would be pretty original, you know what I mean (laughing)? We're using the primary colours, we're using guitar, bass, drums and vocals and we're taking them in a traditional sense, and we're maybe bending that tradition around, we're bringing out the songs."

The importance of the way U-2 evolved their sound is this: that the same open-mindedness, the same willingness to change and develop, the same down to earth understanding of what they are and what they want underlies everything they do. U-2 are searchers. They keep looking. They keep turning over stones.

It goes back a long way. Bono was the first punk in school, a brave step at that time. He turned up one day with a new haircut, tight purple straights, a sixties jacket and a chain leading from his nose to his ear. He was a nice guy but this was something else, stay away from me! The youngest kids were scared, some upset, the teachers in a quandary. His

Larry steps out. Pic: Colm Henry

47

girlfriend broke it off with him! (Soon to be re-united in best Jackie tradition).

Bono is amused by his antics then, but he understands why he did it. "I'll tell you the root of it. I had a feeling that there were things going to happen in music. I had a very strong feeling, and one day I went into the back-room with the band and we talked about this feeling, about a new music that would maybe be rooted in the 60s (I'd been listening to the Beach Boys and Stones). And I felt that and we talked about that, so when I heard "Anarchy In The UK", I mean there it was on the plate. That was exactly what I had been talking about, I went wow! We didn't form because of the Sex Pistols, we were forming at the same time. Except they were 19 and we were 15, and we were like a child who was just learning to walk, we could hardly run! We were falling on our faces, but now we're growing up and we're able to stand firm on what we're doing. But at that stage we were just fumbling around."

"Yeah! I saw punk rock as the real expression of the individual. Just do it! Bring out that side of yourself. I was an extrovert, I am an extrovert, and at that time I was getting a lot of reaction against it. A lot of teachers either hated me or loved me, and the same with other people, and "Anarchy In The UK" inspired me to say right, "Up Your Bum, chum!" do you know what I mean?

"I'd always been interested in 60s clothing because my brother had some, and then in the interest of vibing people up I wore the chain, but that was more for effect than anything. I mean I was like the child who is eating coal. He knows he wants to eat something and I ate the coal and went 'Euuch' ... I realised that it wasn't right for me in some senses. I've made a lot of mistakes like that, but I'm learning."

Bono is at the core of U-2's identity. He bounces off people with an open and direct personality, often talks fast and forcefully, with a speedy urge to express how he feels, is rarely callous or stupid about anyone or anything. He cares about other people, and that is something that has impressed me since I first got to know him. He is a nice human being. A concerned human-being. And lyrically his concern and his questions manifest themselves in a need to understand and express the spiritual aspects of his, of yours and my personality, in as much as he can understand them. This is nothing new, this has been there from the beginning.

In March 1978 in U-2's first Hot Press interview, Bono said to Bill Graham, "Our songs are about different aspects, maybe spiritual, because every teenager, every youth does experience spiritual things, like going to church ... See, I have a problem about things like girls, sex, but we're also dealing with the spiritual ones which

few groups ever touch, even if I know that teenagers do think about these matters."

U-2's first song was "Street Missions": "*I walk tall I walk in a wild wind/I love to start/I love to watch myself grow/Some say maybe tomorrow/Resurrection, Hello/ Oh no no no/Street Missions*".

A confused jumble of words, images, desperation and happiness (this had yet to be arranged), Street Missions was one boy's search for something — '*I need something/I need someone/maybe I need you*' — that pointed the way the group would travel.

Bono is delighted when I mention the song: "This is like my life going before me, I wish people knew what you know. A lot of people will think it's a new thing, but that will prove it."

Throughout their songs U-2 have avoided the beaten track, tacking against the wind into unknown and unusual places. Bono: "I find I write more about the things that *really* concern me, whereas I think a lot of writers write about things they'd *like* to concern them. This Finnish journalist asked me today why I don't write about Northern Ireland, and ... had I thought about it I probably would have, but it *mustn't* concern me that much. I mean it's a very obvious evil, a very obvious problem, but like there's much more, ehm ... unobvious problems which are at the root of that, about people and they concern me."

Bono gets close to The Edge as Larry keeps the beat. Pic: Colm Henry

U-2 have an original sound. Why? They started off playing the same embarrassing cover versions as everyone else; Bay City Rollers songs, "Jumping Jack Flash", "Heart of Gold" (don't blush boys), "Suffragette City", the most appalling version of "Nights In White Satin" you're ever likely to hear anywhere, "2-4-6-8

Bono in the TV Studio. Pic: Colm Henry.

49

1980. Bono looks to the future. Pic: Colm Henry

Motorway", "Anarchy In The UK" ... but they moved from that very rapidly into an area where while that music may have provided the base, the Edge, Adam, Larry and Bono provided the stepping stones. Why did **they succeed in that almost intangible step while others** stumbled into regular routines?

Edge: "Because we could never play any of those songs." Bono: "That's why. We were lousy." Edge: "We were the worst cover version band in the world. *So*, the only way we could actually become good ..." Bono: "Was write our own stuff."

Edge: "I'll tell you exactly what it's like — you're in a French exam and you're trying to do an essay, right? You want to say, ehm 'I was a bit disturbed so I went down to the zoological gardens to eat my lunch'. Oh ... I can't say that, never mind! What you should do is think about what you *can* say, what words you have, and use them, like 'I sat on the chair'."

Bono: "I used to write every single essay about going to the beach. If they asked me about the moon, I'd write 'I went to the moon and discovered a beach!' That's the truth!"

Larry: (laughing) "What's that got to do with anything?"

Edge: "The thing about it is, we broke it down to what we could actually do. From there we started evolving our own songs and as we became better musicians our songs started becoming better. Even our styles started developing around each other, and it was like a continual parallel development, the song, the musicianship and the styles."

Bono: "The way it is is that there's not much music I *do* like, and I realise that our biggest influences are each other. Definitely I can't say specifically how the sound developed. It's like an extension of your personality. You're not always consciously trying to develop something, it just slowly comes out."

From the beginning U-2 have been spurred by a sense of inquiry: from "Twilight's" attempts to understand adolescent growth to "Shadows and Tall Trees" heartbreaking evocation of a sense of wonder, to "Out of Control's" fear of dying, they have constantly looked in as well as out and to a large extent this has been at the core of U-2's appeal. The essential honesty that underlies U-2's existence, and their belief in what they are doing means they must write about it. Their faith exists parallel with their humanity, their care, so there is much to look for in U-2's lyrics, much to lose if you reject them off-hand now.

Bono does not want to talk about his faith, and in many ways that is bad — he is being closeted by what could be a very real rejection by those not willing to tolerate or understand. I don't know how much he would approve of my writing about this now, but I think

50

it is important to say that U-2's involvement with Christianity is not an entirely new thing, merely an extension of the elements of what made you like U-2 in the first place ...

So where do we go from here? Put the pieces together and build up a picture of an album: "Boy". U-2's debut is a crafted, beautiful record, filled with gentle power. It evokes pictures of tainted innocence, snatches at a sense of wonder, is filled with optimism, a positive trust in the values of human nature — it is something which is almost directly opposed to the cynicism and worldliness of modern British rockgroups like Echo and the Bunnymen and the Teardrop Explodes. U-2 celebrate a different set of values.

Bono: "The child on the cover is very important because, like the child, it is very much a beginning for U-2, an introduction to the band. It is slightly retrospective in that we have some of the older material, like "Out of Control" which is two years old, and yet we have lots of other songs like "The Ocean" and "An Cat Dubh" which were three minutes old before we recorded them. I like that about it. It is like a summing up of what we are doing, where we come from and where we are going. I think it's a very important album, as an Irish album, but also as a European album. It doesn't sound like any album that's been coming out of England lately."

Edge: "We did the songs that we felt right with, that fitted in together in a mood, you know, just as songs themselves. We did want an album that worked as a whole, rather than a collection of songs. But that's where the concept ends as an album, but not as Boy, the concept from U-2."

Bono: "Which is there, I mean it's present, but it's locked away in my sub-conscious somewhere, because I don't fully understand it myself. The album cover has been in the back of my mind for two years. There is a feel to the album, holding the cover and listening to the album is perfect, it's a complete bond. But it's been a natural evolution."

Bono and Adam lounge around. Pic: Colm Henry

U-2 believe in their album. They believe in themselves. But this isn't ego-antics, star prancing. Simply belief. People ask if success has changed U-2, or are they still the innocent lads they ever were?

Don't be so bloody silly — everybody changes, time changes everything. Are you the same as you were yesterday? Have you stopped growing already?!?

For the record, Dave is less cocky, more intense; Larry strikes me as nicer, still a little naive but unselfconsciously, very friendly; Adam is wandering about in the background tonight, too vague to get to grips with; Bono is still driven by a vivacious urge to express, but now he is more directed, more sure of exactly what he is trying to say. He believes what he has to say is important, but he avoids a tendency towards self-importance. When I accuse him of crusading in "The Ocean" with the lines "*I thought the world could go far/ If they listened to what I said,*" he denies that implication, though conceding that it is a 'touchy comment'.

"It is just a complete teenage thought, it is the thought of every teenager, it is the thought of everybody in a band who thinks he can change the world. There is another verse which got left out, it's on the sleeve, "*When I looked around/The world couldn't be found/Just me by the sea*', which is the resignation that no matter what you do, people are going to go their own way."

But don't confuse self-importance with self-confidence because U-2 are bubbling over with that. Bono: "The band isn't gonna stop. You've seen the pits, you've seen where we've come from, you've seen the child eating the coal. To get from there to here you'll admit is rather interesting, to get from here to a gold album in the US is nothing, a small step. I'm serious, we're gonna break America like no British band has broken it in a long time. We go over to the US, things are happening. This guy from Premier Talent is the biggest booking agent in the world. He books Springsteen, the Who, etc., he broke Zeppelin and the Who in the US. He has picked up on this band before we released our 1st album in the US! He's turned down The Boomtown Rats but took us up on the strength of our album. The smallest bands he's had, apart from us, are the B52's, who've had a hit album in the States and the Pretenders, who've had a number one album! That jump is made, Frank Barcelona from Premier Talent has gotten behind us and believes that we are the band to do it. So Warners, WEA in the US have taken us *very* seriously. We were going to be released on Island in the US but Warners want us. This *Rolling Stone* journalist was sent over to talk to us. *The New York Rocker* was over today. People are talking about this band, this band that aren't self-indulgent like most British bands, which aren't putting it out, They're gonna want us in the US."

Me: "Why is it so important that U-2 should be so successful?"

Bono: "Why? Because music can be a celebration of life. It's like a contemporary art-form for *everybody*, working class or upper-class. Never before has there been an art-form so versatile, and it's being abused, it's being commercialised and it's being bent. The punk thing was trying to straighten that out, but as usual power corrupts and it bent it out worse than it was in the first place. I think it's important that U-2 are recognised because we're standing against that, it's one up for the positive side of the pop-culture.

"I think if we are number one we're doing people like Rush out of a place, if we're on the radio we're doing people like Sheena Easton out of a job — a factory product. They might be nice people but I don't like that attitude, a tin of beans, a tin of music, dress it up and launch it?!"

So stop and listen! Wrap them up and take them home, this package of U-2, this tin of music, put them on the cooker and watch them explode! Nurture them carefully and learn to share in their heart and soul. Care about them, because they deserve your care and attention. Don't elevate them, talk to them. Don't *admire* them, like them. U-2 are a very, very special group, and maybe I am too caught up in them to cast an outsider's glance at what they do, but I've got something an outsider hasn't found yet.

U-2 take my breath away. I knew you'd understand. ∎

Neil McCormick
Vol 4 No. 15
December 17th, 1980

U2 Could Be in L.A.

Charlie McNally sees U2 launch their U.S. invasion.

U-2 AT the most prestigious venue in Los Angeles were only dynamite — I can put it no more succinctly than that. For the past ten days I've been listening to KROQ 106.7 FM (Dave Fanning beware!) which, incidentally, is *the* new wave station of Southern California, and they've been paving the way for the assault on LA by those new darlings of the British rock press, U-2.

Island-Warners seems to be throwing some weight and a few bucks behind the whole thing — the approach to the tour positively bristles with activity, organisation promotion and all the other on-the-road related jive, e.g. a SPACE BUS which sleeps most everyone. I mean, you can piss and shower in it, keep the champagne cold, watch TV and the sound system within is astounding — all this is in the capable hands of a certain Mr. Joe O'Herlihy from Cork.

Promoting concerts in Los Angeles is a tough ol' business but The Country Club has quickly become a top live music, liggin' joint, concert club in LA, featuring a great variety of music from new wave to country. Record execs abound, hand out their cards, tellin' you who they are and what they do and talking million dollar deals. The sunny, tanned women (oh those California girls) wear designer jeans and almost up-to-date hairstyles. As Vidal Sassoon says on the radio: "If you don't look good, we don't look good". He charges forty bucks.

The metropolis of Los Angeles is the melting pot of the world — it's all things to all people. Hollywood, the tinsel-town, attracts many of the most talented people in search of success in movies, music or fashion, which are very much interrelated industries. Some make money in such quantities it's hard to comprehend, others fulfil their dreams, but many leave disappointed and disillusioned. Life is lived in the fast lane — and I mean on the right hand side of the road but in the left hand lane, in fifth gear at whatever speed outruns the cops, ha! People work hard but play hard too.

Well, out came the Qualudes, the Cocaine and the best California Pot you ever did see, as the elite new wave rich kids and the record execs I mentioned earlier, welcomed, politely at first, U-2 in the debut appearance on the West Coast, US of A.

The Country Club was warm but not too hot; the day

had been in the low 70's — a nice climate, pleasant on the mind 'n' senses. The boys had a swim in the Marquis pool and a dip in the jacuzzi — a great way to start the day, but there was a gig to get together, so John Kennedy, Tim Nicholson, Joe O'Herlihy and Paul arrived at the venue at 2 pm. as arranged, only to find the place closed and gig people unavailable (they were all down at the Long Beach Grand Prix, 40 miles away). So the pressure was on and the pace began to heat up as sound check and AOK were necessary before 7 pm — but like any good road crew that knows its shit, these guys were ready.

Now, the Country Club is *the* showcase gig in LA of everyone from local hot shots Naughty Sweeties to Ry Cooder — but U-2 took the place by storm. There was a sense of anticipation in the room, which holds about 1000 people, prior to the show, reflecting the fact that many had advance knowledge of this "young band" from Dublin.

The set opened slowly and tentatively as the band settled in and checked out the audience who, by the way, had come to watch and listen not to spit, fight or pogo. I immediately realised that this was a *new band*, one that had been knocked into shape by many long days on the road — a far cry from the day that young Paul Hewson (Bono to you) asked me on College Green if his band could play support "for nothin'" on the Greedies' gig at the Stardust in Artane. Little did I think that only two years later I'd witness that same band playin' their asses off in Sunny California.

Most of the material was plucked from their debut "Boy" album which originally entered the US charts at 98 with a double bullet and has continued to rise since. Gems like "Out Of Control", "Stories For Boys", "Day Without Me", and "Boy Girl", were the high points in a very professional, almost polished, stage show — probably not as flashy as Hollywood would want, but excellent in an earthy Irish way which, of course, was well received.

I'm not going to criticise the set in the manner of yer average rock journalist — tight sound, stupendous lighting etc. yawn! turn to p. 94. Suffice to say the final twenty minutes were exceptional in that U-2 actually managed to rouse those bored Los Anglicans who sat up and took notice — they even called for two encores. Mr. Edge played some inspired guitar and Adam decked in

America: Adam ponders his next move. Pic: Adrian Boot.

headband "fer de swea", pumped out a wild bass. Bono moved and pranced around stage (who's his choreographer?) with great ease and confidence — too much echo on his vocals but the skins were just perfect. There is a discipline and maturity about U-2 hithertofore unseen in Irish bands and I hope, indeed believe, that this band is going all the way to the top of the international ladder.

The after-gig lig was as expected — an efficiently organised affair in the reception room, short and sweet so that such 'n' such could meet such 'n' such and exchange cards and numbers and gossip: "I met someone who went out with Warren Beatty, you know", or as this German starlet beside me says "Ve shaal all go back to my hows an'/ze jacuzzi sheal give much pleasure, JA?" Much imbibing took place.

Anyhow, Bono and the boys saw pretty quickly what was goin' down, put in a quiet and restrained appearance, answered a few questions and soon headed back to LA's rock 'n' roll hotel the Sunset Marquis, which is situated near Barney's Beanery, a Pool 'n' Food 'n' Beer joint of repute, frequented by many a transient rock 'n' roller. Then, of course, there's the glitter of the Rainbow just up on Sunset Strip where all drinks are two bucks fifty and the girls are just beootiful. Sunset is renowned as the best hooker street, but Santa Monica Blvd., running parallel is great for little boys! Wealth and decadence are inseparable. Anyone who saw TV in the late fifties might remember the Vegas-type of detective series called "77 Sunset Strip", — well, it still exists but is now a striptease joint with a huge overhead sign saying "Guaranteed totally nude or double your money back". It sums up the way this town ticks, i.e. money screams, guarantees are necessary, efficiency and The Ultimate are the goal. That mood didn't phase U-2 ...

Tonight I had the pleasure of observing a tiny paragraph in Irish rock music history — U-2's debut in LA — so I thought I'd send you these few words for the record. "Keeping the world (Ireland) safe for Rock 'n' Roll" etc ... ∎

Charlie McNally

Vol 5 No. 7 April 17th, 1981

A shoe-shine for Bono. Pic: Adrian Boot

U2 Versus the U.S.

Bono jumps across America. Pic: Adrian Boot.

Bill Graham joins the band on their 1981 American tour.

Eight miles high and then I touch down, go through immigration at Chicago's O'Hare Airport and, hey, it's the Edge all on his owneo. "Bill how are you? Nice to see you" he greets me, attired in sloppy jeans and jacket, most unbecomingly unlike what Americans expect in their rock stars. Turns out he's waiting here for his girl-friend Aisling, who's meant to be on the same flight as *mise*.

"I didn't see her" I tell him, explaining that she was probably grounded by the same morning fog at Dublin Airport, meaning that she's also missed her connection at London and, like me, will arrive a day later than planned (which is exactly what happens).

Such schedule-scrambling means that I've lost a day's acclimatising cure for jet-lag and must muck into U-2's American tour, hoping that my mind and body will improvise sufficient of a working relationship to let me attend to both the business and pleasure of the assignment.

But that flight. Not eight but six miles high (who am I to spoil a good introduction?) over Greenland, a worthy burgher two rows behind me is taken with a severe angina attack and, until three flying doctors appear to calm both his condition and my and the other passenger's anxieties, I'm fearing that someone just ten feet away is going to die on me (you get very selfish at 34,000 feet) whilst simultaneously I'm panicking as to what the next reel of this disaster movie will bring.

Not the most soul-settling introduction to America. When the Jumbo lands at Chicago, I and I are hardly talking to each other. Excuse me while I collapse into the next paragraph ...

America — yes you'll find that it's stranger than Nome. But I don't intend to log a pat tourist's summary — "America: Its Myths, Mores And Mince Beef" — since I've already suffered through my share of London journalists' instant commentaries on Ireland.

Instead let's just stick with music, specifically U-2 and their campaign in the mid-west through Chicago, Cincinnati and Detroit — here, rather than the coastal cities, because this is where the real touring drudgery occurs, here in its heartlands where America finally decides which acts it will accept.

U-2 have already impacted on the coasts. As I arrive, "Boy" is at 63 in the *Billboard* charts, a stirring performance for a first album. From an English vantage point, U-2's chart achievements here — ahead of both 1980's Top of the Bopsters and the Liverpool bands with whom they're constantly associated — may seem anachronistic, given that the patchy sales of "Boy" — strong in London and the north-west, weak elsewhere — ensured that it never entered the British charts. Yet there are strong reasons, business, artistic and ultimately sheer attitudinal, why U-2 are so successfully splashing in the American pool.

Business first. By signing to Island, U2 filled an important and till then vacant niche in the company's roster. Ever since Eddie and The Hot Rods crumpled, Island lacked an identifiable modern rock band. Indeed they had Bob Marley and dance-masters like the B-52's, Grace Jones and Robert Palmer but anyone who remembers Island's line-up circa '73 will recognise how tilted their collection of acts had become. Certainly such appears to have been the opinion of their American distributors Warner Brothers.

The Burbank Brothers Warner indeed. If a band has their promotional engine powering the machine, first flight is so much easier. U-2 have been awarded a national promotional priority by Warners, the same treatment that has just guided Stevie Winwood's "Arc Of A Diver" album to number 1. Nobody in the band or the record company expects any such immediate dizzy fame — U-2 are still putting their name about — but the band can tour without watching their backs for morale-deflecting seizures in their plans and so confidently concentrate on their music.

Finally U-2 are booked by Premier Talent, the most experienced agency in the business. Under Premier's patronage, U-2 have as human-suited a schedule as can be organised in America. No playing in toilets, no tiring cross-country night-flights, U-2 may not travel in style but they do tour according to a logical plan.

Manager Paul McGuinness is most proud of the coup, as also his timing since he won over the agency before he contacted American Warners for their support — thereby persuading the record company of U-2's serious intent towards America. McGuinness doesn't have much regard for the manner in which many English managements approach America. Unsentimentally he believes they disguise their failures in understanding the States by allowing their bands to propandise about their artistic integrity and American intolerance — in short the Strangler's "Americans have smaller brains" syndrome. He may have a point.

But the noise! U-2 may suit America because these continentals prefer their bands to be positive,

Larry, Adam and Bono go shopping in The States. Pic: Adrian Boot

extroverted and dramatic. U-2's current weaknesses in terms of passing British fashions — middle-class art bands must be inward and moody, working-class bands must dance to a revival beat — are reversed into strengths trans-Atlantic. 2-Toners cause too many translation difficulties and the New Romantics may be too delicately reserved for American tastes, also perhaps a whit condescending.

Ultimately it's a matter of attitude. Many English bands seem uneasy about their American appeal and almost boast of their failure there, as if it were a badge of honour, possibly fearing that U.S. success would stigmatise them in the eyes of their home fans. Being Irish, U-2 have no such insecurities and aren't automatically conscripted to take sides in the trans-

Atlantic cultural war. Mid-way through each set, Bono tells his audience, "We're not just another English band passing through. We're Irish (pause) ... and we're in your country for three months."

The Yanks generally see the point of his sentiments.

So having imbibed all such relevant information in Paul McGuinness's room at Chicago's Holiday Inn, I'm hauled off to U-2's university gig tonight. I try to relax but hadn't reckoned with a Palestinian taxi driver who monologues about the struggle of his people with Israel. I'm wearily content to play the standard Irish anti-colonial role — our lads in Lebanon, the possibility of a P.L.O. office in Dublin — but McGuinness counters the

U2 go to the movies. Pic: Adrian Boot

cabbie's case.

"Don't you think" he inquires, "the reason the Jews are so stubborn is that six million of them, more than you've yet lost, were killed in concentration camps during the war?"

"Oh no, that's just Zionist propaganda," answers our driver, "it is only about 200,000."

He continues to rifle out his opinions faster than Garret Fitzgerald on speed. McGuinness bargains him up to half-a-million but my paranoia rating has shot through the roof. Already I've caught a severe case of America. Wheel me out, get me to the gig!

Which is rather disappointing. My own disorientation certainly contributes but U-2 and their student audience don't mesh till the final stretch before the encore. The crowd comprises solely students, with a sizeable minority just out for a night's cruising and boozing whoever be the band and U-2 seem to recognise this: they don't seem to be playing on full power till near the close. I only become attuned during Bono's routines in "Boy Girl" when the front rows fling up a salvo of cigarettes for his nervous teenager act and he wildly flexes his palm over the spluttering lighter. He's acclaimed, a clue granted as to the U-2 chutzpah with which Americans identify.

Otherwise all I remember is the local Warners promotion person who compares The Edge's guitar

with Duane Eddy. Or was it Link Wray? Anyway, it was one of those nights. I take a body count.

At this point a wise man would have slid between the sheets but my medical advisers tell me that the best cure for jet-lag is to hammer the body into submission, forcing its rhythms into American time. So we go out clubbing.

I have professional reasons. Echo and The Bunnymen are playing at Tut's, a downtown club so there are comparisons to be made between U-2's fortunes and theirs. The word in the U-2 camp, said without any gloating, is that The Bunnymen aren't enjoying the smoothest of tours. Despite being signed to Warners, they are a secondary priority behind U-2 and a later investigation of an American radio playlist directory shows how little airtime the Bunnymen are receiving.

Indeed there are rumours that American Warners won't pick up the option to release their second album in the States, an indication of how harshly the American machine can react if it's encountered unprepared. At Tut's, The Bunnymen are booked to play two lengthy sets, a commitment U-2 have so far avoided on this tour. Verily fates and methods are contrasting.

Bono and the band go backstage to talk with them, the singer being set on mediating in the **Crucial Three**

60

feud between Ian McCullough and Wah!'s Pete Wylie. I settle on watching the local support to learn about American waves.

Well I don't know how representative they are but I trust there are better bands in Chicago. What's offered is efficient posturing, crisp industrious riff-rock from a band so determined to sell themselves that they've mislaid their soul.

They have a chick singer — and when I say a "chick" singer, I mean a "chick" singer — garbed in black tights and regimented as a platinum plastic fantastic lover. The Jenny Darren revival starts here and when she and the guitarist mime sexual assault, they do it so ineptly I immediately flash on The Prunes.

Such automatic music immediately stimulates one sub-theme of the trip. Questions, questions. Why are American bands so elderly? Why can't the kids in America play for themselves? What chance does a highschool band, a potential U-2, have in the States?

I'm still pondering when Bono slips beside me to hawk-eyedly watch Echo. I do my best and my few antennae that are still working order me they're good but their set seems interminable, a conspiracy solely aimed at preventing my exhausted body find sleep. So long Bunnymen, I think I met you on a grouchy night!

Next night I'm feeling less like I'm still cruising at 30,000 feet each time my feet touch the pavement. U-2 play the Park West, a club that is what the Venue should be. Warmly hospitable, an excellent sound system and with a democratic layout that discriminates against no spectator, the Park West does not follow an exclusive New Wave (U.S. record company term) policy, having featured Don McLean the preceding night. U-2's appearance there is further corroboration of their refusal to be shoved into any newly-developed rock ghetto.

Their advance reputation and the grinding of Warners' promo mills have filled the club to its 1,100 plus capacity and now that Bono has an audience to play with, the set is several notches superior to yesterday's.

Playing America, U-2 have to be more explicit, highlight their main features and shadow the subtleties. I have to keep reminding myself that virtually everyone in this hall has never encountered them live before and that the lines of communication therefore are routed towards the innocent.

Their 50-minute set is essentially based round the album, opening with the casually self-effacing and thus proud "The Ocean", revving upward with "11 O'Clock Tick Tock" and then smouldering into "An Cat Dubh", U-2's invitation to majesty that silkily ties the bonds between band and audience. Tonight, there is reception, the audience scrappily clapping along to The Edge's guitar hymn. From then on out, U-2 have lift-off, Paul

Bono meets Sting!! Pic: Adrian Boot

McGuinness pronounces it one of those rare champagne concerts and Bono feigns inability as he struggles to screw off the cork. Chicago, it's their kind of town!

But settled in my plush seat, I can't endorse their manager's judgement. I'm happy because U-2 are happy but there the circle stops. I'm intellectually appreciative of the entertainment but still unmoved by jet-lag and my severe case of America-itis. As the promotion persons and the disc jockeys press the flesh in the dressing-room, I conspire to get back on the road again.

In the Mid-West, American radio is worse than even this pessimist feared. When U-2 play Cincinnati, their album stands at 29 according to national radio play rating, figures created by the airtime they're winning on the coasts and in certain regional pockets. So a logical human specimen would expect such ratings to be reflected by Cincinnati's rock media, particularly since they are about to play their debut concert in the city.

Not so. Except for some low-powered college stations, U-2 have been non-persons on Cincinnati's radio dials and even though they pull 800 to Bogart's club and send them home happy, they can't anticipate more than a minor presence on the listings.

Or take Detroit, the next leg of the trip. There U-2 haul in 1,400 to Harpo's, again without benefit of any commercial airplay whatsoever in a city twice the size of Dublin. Pause and reconsider oh ye Comsat Angels and Altered Images, ye Bush Tetras and Raybeats!

Warners' Detroit promotion man has tagged along with the music directors of the main stations but even after an excellent show they're still saying "no commitments Bob" and he has no idea if they've been persuaded.

But then Detroit may be the Black Hole of radio — or so I'm informed. In the last six months, a new station has opened up whose performing policy is to rotate only eight album acts, these being such mastodons as Styx, R.E.O. Speedwagon and Led Zeppelin (Jimmy Page's problem — how to be Aleister Crowley in Scotland and a hamburger in Detroit!). This institution of cultural extermination has achieved such an audience rating that its Detroit competitors are running scared, restricting and imploding their playlists. I'm told that even such a doughtily conservative outfit as Aerosmith are meeting resistance from programmers.

What such blackouts indicate is that even if the American music industry implemented all the intelligent reforms Robert Fripp and others advocate, the impact could be minimal due to radio oppression. One can't escape the tragic fact that American radio, increasingly owned by conglomerates with no vocational interest in broadcasting, is not interested in the welfare of the native

music industry. In so many cities, it is exclusively — and I mean exclusively — interested in its own profit margins. American radio holds a bull-terrier's grip on the jugular of the nation's popular taste.

Fortunately Chicago isn't such a desert. The afternoon after the Park West date, Adam Clayton taxies out to the city's proper rock station W-'XMET, accompanied by producer Steve Lillywhite who's joined partly to holiday, partly to supervise material for the second album. There they meet disc-jockey Bobby Skafish (for trivialists, cousin of Skafish who had an album out on Illegal last year) for an interview. Here's some of what they told Chicago — here's how U-2 promote themselves to Middle America.

Skafish: At the show, Bono made a remark that you're not just another English touring band. Do you have an interpretation on that?

Clayton: What Bono was trying to say is that we are putting a certain amount of energy and commitment into the United States. We're not just coming over because we have to tour because our record company says so. We actually enjoy America. We're not here to slag it off or say America stinks and they don't listen to good music. We're actually feeling very good about America and we want to be here and we want to put that commitment down and work that hard. That's the point he's making.

Skafish: There's a tendency in a band touring in your

> **"We actually enjoy America. We're not here to slag it off or say America stinks and they don't listen to good music. We're actually feeling good about America, we want to be here and we want to put that commitment down and work that hard." — Adam**

situation to be treated as the one after Echo and The Bunnymen and the one before Adam and The Ants?

Clayton: I think there is that danger but I like to think we have more identity than that. In many ways, people find it difficult to group us in with other acts like that — because we do define our own territory to a large extent.

In many ways America is different because you don't have the nationwide press that you have in England which is where such thoughts and ideas come from. So people are basically hearing about U-2 on the radio and going to gigs so they can't really link it in with anything that has been experienced in England. To them, it's totally new rock and roll. And that's important. That's the way we should be viewed.

Skafish: What about the way that bands can be subjected to criticism for trying to get out of their own little corner of the world? The Clash are probably the best example of that, a band who took criticism for playing to the United States. I gather from you, your attitude is: It's a big world, let's go after it.

Clayton. Yeah. Obviously you've got certain standards and ambitions which you set yourself and which you wish to attain within a given time. Progress is what stimulates the creative juices.

Skafish: Reading some of your press, I get a sense of mission with your touring. It's not a standard "We'll break the album, we'll go home, we'll establish our market". There's a little bit more, farther-reaching ramifications.

Clayton: In a way we've taken quite a serious commitment. We're here for three months which is very unusual for a non-American band. We're encouraged because we're getting good reactions.

At the same time, we feel and I think many others feel that things are going to change in America musically. I don't think it's going to continue much longer with very strict radio programming and very, like, middle of the road, and R.E.O. Speedwagon, very bland type of music.

Skafish: You're speaking in their home town, I'll have you know.

Clayton: Oh, shake them up a bit ...

Skafish: Have you written the second album?

Clayton: Steve Lillywhite is in America now to make us do the work (laughs). We've got the songs in rough form. But it basically needs us all sitting down and being a bit disciplined about it and actually shaping them up into songs.

Lillywhite: I don't think they will be as shaped as the first album at the start.

Clayton: I think there's going to be a lot more air in the next recording. At least this is what he tells me.

Skafish: Where are you going to record?

Clayton: We're going to record in Dublin again. We've got a great studio there and we're all very relaxed and happy there and we're all in love with the studio manager.

Cincinnati is just so much more pleasant. After Chicago's gusty bleak spaces and intimidating skyscrapers, it's a Kentucky sunshine drive from the airport across the Ohio river to a student suburb where the main street buildings are no more than two storeys and the food is edible (no more Holiday Inn jellied Kleenex). I breathe.

You too U-2 — the girl-friends have arrived. Aisling

Adam takes one way to the top. Pic: Adrian Boot

has been with The Edge since Chicago but now there's Ali for Bono and Annie for Larry. Guess who they'll be playing to impress tonight! Lucky Cincinnati!

I know it's a great set because super-fan Larry Mullen is smiling. This fan's rule for U-2 is that if Larry is grinning, the band must be enjoying themselves and if the band are ...

I figure Bono's amended the words of "An Cat Dubh" for Ali and there's probably all sorts of by-ray going down I don't understand, but the romance takes hold and all the worries that nudged me in Chicago are dissolved and I put them down to the jet-lag. Hey, it's *my* champagne gig! Damn, Bogart's don't have any! Nor even sparkling white either! What do ya mean bartender, will red wine do?

No champagne in Cincinnati but in the most intimate hall of the tour, it's my favourite. Just like Chicago, they earn two encores and when I go back to the dressingroom, I'm spouting praise left, right and centre.

"That was almost as good as Chicago" says The Edge.

"Oh ... well ... I ..."

Adam escapes the attention of two ladies who tell him they drink much milk and wine and we retreat back to the tour bus, lazily rapping with fans on the balmy street. I slip into the back compartment of the tourer, check out their tapes and see the light.

Or rather a copy of "The Byrds Greatest Hits". "Oh yeah, we got that when we started the tour," roadie Pod says.

Time to think dizzy thoughts. Lazy writers in the American press have lumped U-2 together with the Liverpool bands in a "psychedelic revival". I can't speak for the Liverpudlians but U-2 have never given any forethought to the matter. Bono does have a Love compilation but he only picked it up after U-2's sound was patented. Somehow through the Edge, they just stumbled on a sound that is the other side of '66 from The Jam.

Still The Byrds ... They do share the same rush ... The first record I ever bought was a CBS sampler with "Eight Miles High" ... It's your favourite track of the moment, Edge? Roger McGuinn knows of you, really? ... And what's that you're saying Edge?

"I'm buying a twelve-string."

En route to Detroit, and the Ohio countryside from the bus looks like a giant golf course. "The road is the fairway" adds Steve Lillywhite.

Up front are himself, Tim Nicholson, Joe O'Herlihy and John Kennedy of the crew, Ellen Dorst of Warners who's taking care of city-to-city promotion, absorbedly knitting, driver Bill, his girlfriend Sue, and Adam.

Back are The Secret Six plus Pod, sleeping, lazily chatting and generally just sharing the moment that they're together in America, wheeling down the road and that all bets on dreams are still on.

Interlude. Peace. Dreams.

No interference.

Did you call that car of mine a cab?" "Whaa ..." Turn slowly, what's the fury? We've just left the Detroit Holiday Inn after Bono has taped a cable TV interview and suddenly there's this angry, really angry, freak who looks like he's had a psychedelic revival of his own from alcohol and/or whatever synthetic substances he's ingested.

"Did you call that car of mine a cab, you muthafucker?"

Fortyish, denims, leather boots, trailing grey hair and glasses, looking for a No K Corral. He's pointing at Bono.

"Ah well, he meant a Cadillac." Translation difficulties we hope.

"Look there may be a police station over there but I don't CAAAHERR. Hey you" — he points at one of the television crew — "I don't like people who wear white shoes".

Steve Lillywhite and Adam on the American airwaves. Pic: Adrian Boot

Paranoia, Knives, guns in the afternoon? Back in the car, his two schoolmarmish passengers look flustered. To his right, one foot away and six inches beneath him, Bono stands immobile. Watching the hands?

We mumble our excuses and flee. Bono is innocent.

"Well I walked out there before you did and he called me a faggot. I wasn't going to walk away. Sure I knew it was a Cadillac, sure I called it a cab. It was strange. I had emotions then I didn't wish to think I still had."

Detroit (panic in).

We've got to get there early. They're booing the support band." Tim Nicholson fears we're about to wander into an audience riot and a canned support band at Harpo's, the Detroit club on the outskirts of a black ghetto that's tonight's assignment.

He's over-anxious. The support, a crew of cover-merchants, are sprinting through their Led Zeppelin replays without pausing for introductions that might provoke the audience who are now suffering through their second such set of the night. They survive but yet again I'm crestfallen by the support bands I've seen on this leg of the tour. Somewhere beyond, there must be imaginative daring young bands who don't make a fetish of "tightness" and who don't make vices of secondary virtues.

But the structure of Mid-Western rock appears calculated to debar youth. Oppressive radio that won't sponsor local records, the surfeit of aged bar bands (or so it seems) who should give up but instead infest the spaces young bands require and drinking laws against under-21's which don't encourage club-owners to book younger bands — for all these reasons, the Mid-West discriminates against teenage expression. If there's a would-be U-2 out there in some Michigan high school, they've probably given up through frustration.

U-2 finally appear and confirm my view that they've gained so much poise. Hardly a year ago in London, you could fear for Bono, but now he's gained control without sacrificing convictions. Then he could too eagerly chivvy an audience, now he's learnt how to persuade them.

Detroit is the longest set I witness, U-2 slipping in the instrumental "Things To Make And Do" and a new song conditionally titled "Fall" that has some of the chugging road rhythms of America. Remarkably there are some Irish fans present who offer up a white sheet, smeared with an "Up The Dubs" slogan. Bono wraps it around him.

U-2 persuade the Motor City audience to three encores, symmetrically finishing as they do all sets with "11 O'Clock" and "The Ocean". The largest crowd with the least pre-publicity, the strongest response, it has been the most profitable date I've seen.

In the dressing room, the pressure has finally fallen on Bono and he quits to a private corner when the business well-wishers arrive. His voice has become huskier each day since Chicago but that affliction is a welcome excuse for someone who tonight can't handle another round of ritual hand-shaking. The other three represent the band but they're happier talking with the few fans who slip through the security cordon.

In any other city in any other country, this concert

66

Hanging around on streets corners! Pic: Adrian Boot

would be accounted a triumph yet U-2 could still be on the outside, their record company still pleading for airplay. Such cultural suffocation — Bono retires. He needs to breathe deep, very very deep.

With Bono's voice in such disrepair, we've left the interview till the last possible moment. He's still croaking the next morning but at least he has the knowledge that after three more dates, the band take their first break in three months when they fly to the Bahamas for a holiday.

I flash on the comparison between Irish showbands and the Mid-West megabands. On a higher dimension, U-2 are fighting a similar struggle. Detroit could be a larger Limerick. He doesn't disagree with my theme, though he diplomatically refuses to upset the Limerick jury by accepting my comparison of cities. But he quickly moves to a more positive line.

"The audience are open in themselves but because of the conservatism of the media due to advertising — because the radio depends on this — it's a lowest common denominator and they're not giving songs a chance to mature.

"It's a battle. The people who are in the streets need to hear it and the only way of being able to change that is by getting the radio programmers to change and the only way to get them to change is to get them to see us face to face. We're over there knocking on doors hard and if you have to come back a second time, a third time, a fourth time, a fifth time, those radio stations will fall because when they come down and see a place like last night, a huge place basically sold out and there's been no radio play, they start thinking — what is this?

"Also they still have the bad taste of punk rock in their mouth. And anything that has any resemblance frightens them because change frightens those people, and they've got this industry sewn up. So the idea is to sit on change.

"But if they see all those people squashed up into this hall, giving, applauding, it starts to make them think — well hold on, we're being left behind."

Just like Adam Clayton, Bono will argue that American music is about to improve. "I really think something is about to happen. The idea of an explosion in 1976 has been somewhat delayed. I think it's happening now." And in earlier chats, he speaks of bands in Washington D.C., Texas and a San Francisco band, Romeo Void, with whom they've been particularly taken. Perhaps such optimism isn't induced by their own euphoria and I've just tripped through the glummest region of America. I sincerely hope so.

Bono accepts that they run a potentially disturbing gauntlet by playing to audiences older than themselves but again he refers back to early Irish experiences.

"It reminded me of the Baggot Inn last night. I mean we were 18 years old and there were people outside who couldn't get in because they were under-age so there were fifty people turned away one night.

"We've been touring six months now ... we chose to do that because U2 could be misinterpreted as a group and we feel the only way to lay a foundation for us to grow on is to play to people face to face and let them make up their mind." — Bono

"We're playing to audiences older than ourselves and it hasn't changed, nothing's changed. It's like bees around honey all those people — they see excitement, something moving. Personally if I don't feel ready for it, I opt out — just like last night in the dressing room."

Wasn't that a small example of how such pressurised American touring can weaken the will? Don't you have to keep catching yourself?

"You caught me catching myself last night and that's a process I know I go through and each member of the band goes through every week. We've been touring six months now with three weeks off. We chose to do that. We don't have record companies telling us to do that. It's the other way round and we have chosen to do that because U-2 could be misinterpreted as a group and we feel the only way to lay a foundation for us to grow on, is to play to people face to face and let them make up their mind.

"That's why we toured for three months in England. That's why we started off in the pits in the Hope and Anchor and worked our way up to the Lyceum, that's why we did it in Europe, in Germany playing beer kellers right up to cinemas and that's exactly what, on a different level, we're doing here except that we're starting much higher — but we have to *get* higher because it's a bigger country.

"I think in many ways the Americans are innocent and more honest than us. They're very wide-eyed, it seems, but they make up their minds by instinct and I think that's very healthy. The reason that music is stale over here is that they haven't been given a chance to let their instinct go to work. But when it does, it sparks."

Sure but they can be misled into expecting juvenile hippies when so much Mid-American press is touting you as part of a psychedelic revival?

"I think people who are using that term are people who are inarticulate and who can't explain what we're doing. Anyone who comes from Dublin can cope with that because they know us and they know what we've been doing over the years. It's just that in America they're only meeting us this year, so they think maybe this band sat down and worked on a psychedelic revival."

In this Holiday Inn restaurant, we're about to sign off and stop the tape but the husky-voiced Bono is insistent on one last message.

"You must mention the family arrangement in the bus between Joe O'Herlihy, John Kennedy, Pod and Tim and the fact that there was somebody born during the tour.

"Joe O'Herlihy's wife bore a daughter in Cork. I think that's very important.

"And we apply that arrangement to everybody, management, record company, agency and gradually the whole unit is getting bigger and stronger. We're standing on our own two feet and gradually getting more mature.

"Last night I could have turned to Ellen Darst and said "Ellen, I want those people out" and she would have — and we've done it before but we're getting that power and that control.

"This unit is getting stronger and working and at the top of it are four people who may be twenty years old and there's all those people 30, 34, all their jobs depending on it and that's an interesting situation coming from 10 Cedarwood Road. And there's literally millions of dollars at stake.

"And there's all these people hustling around you and I can see how people are sucked in. It's so easy because there becomes this complete wall around you, of people who think you're great.

"There's just one final thing I want to say. This touring. We've beaten it, it hasn't beaten us. We're not going out like a showband, playing tra-la-la every night."

The bus is leaving for their next appointment in Columbus, Ohio. I shake hands all round, wave goodbye and muse in the Holiday Inn's forecourt, all forebodings diminished and dismissed.

So far U-2 have retained immunity, so far U-2 have made no pacts with the devils. Clear-sightedly and with total commitment, they're taking on America the only way it can be conquered. You cannot afford waste or sloth, you cannot permit distraction, you cannot condescend and you must purge yourself of pre-conceptions.

The bus drives South. Hello Columbus. ∎

Bill Graham
Vol 5 No. 8 May 1st, 1981

U2 and crew with Bill Graham second from right in the front row.   Pic: Adrian Boot

Autumn Fire

Neil McCormick reviews "October".

A CELEBRATION is in order. A smile, a tear, an emotional response to an emotional situation. To passionate friends: this music gives birth to a swelling gladness within me. U-2 have kept a promise.

That U-2 are important to me, to a lot of people reading and writing for *Hot Press* and to many more besides cannot (nor should it need to) be denied. The reasons why they are important should be understood. It begins with their music which has a power to move that most rock music has forgotten; it is the guitar chords U-2 strike within you; U-2 really do play their songs in the key of life. It is the life within the group, the people, their personalities, their skills, the combination that makes them special.

But caring about a group does not mean you must be blind to their faults. U-2's debut LP "Boy" was a magnificent record, epic in scope and personal in touch. I waited for their second LP. I worried slightly, and finally "October" came. I played it and felt "good". And that reaction was disappointing. A week later the LP has grown and grown, expanding towards "great", rushed on by the explosion of superlatives. Celebrate!

From the growing cry of the opening song "Gloria", from a wistful echo to a glorious shout, it is made clear that U-2 have at last *openly* embraced in their music the Christian faith that has been running in more subtle form through the lyrics of "I Will Follow", "An Cat Dubh", and "Shadows ..." and which has been the mainstay of three members' lives, singer Bono, guitarist The Edge and drummer Larry. "We don't want to be the band that talks about God," said Bono at the end of last year. So instead they sing about God. *"O Lord, if I had anything/Anything at all/I'd give it to you"* he sings on "Gloria". What they have is their music ...

"October" is a Christian LP. People will react to this fact in different ways: snide, disappointed, alienated, unconcerned, overtly happy. I accept it because at the core of U-2 is honesty, and therefore, the only way their music can continue to be successful is if they are honest. And honesty is ...

"I try to stand up but I can't find my feet/I try to speak up but only in you I am complete/Gloria in eo Domine".

Bono at Slane Castle, 1981. Pic: Colm Henry

"October" is a musical and spiritual growth for U-2, a passionate and moving LP for me. U-2 have evolved constantly, songs changing and growing over a period of time. "Boy" was an incredibly impressive LP because it caught a group who had grown for five years. "October" is the product of one more year, and so it isn't a leap into the unknown, rather a step forward, and a refinement of ideas.

Musically, The Edge's picturesque playing improves as time gives him the skills to equal his imagination. The guitars throughout are superb; slicing, scratching, charging, plunking, always echoing the song's feel. Larry's drumming has taken a plunge off the high-diving board of possibilities, integrating discords, funk, Phil Collins thudding patternwork and things that go bump in the dark, making the drums the most immediately impressive part of the sound. Adam's basswork remains simplistic, but he too has taken new funk rhythms in his stride, adding twists that are, as ever, a fully integrated part of the whole. And Bono's singing has become more confidently modulated, capable of being harder and softer without cracking. Lyrically he has become more basic, without losing his flights of almost subconscious poetry — his words still provide the basis of a picture, which the group and listener fill in.

"October" divides into its two sides, together making up a unified whole. Side one is the most immediately

---

"'October' is an LP of exciting, emotional, spiritually inclined rock. The most uplifting rock LP of the year 'October' is a modern dance that studies no trends, relies on no false aura of cool."

---

impressive, opening up with the inspiring "Gloria" and continuing through four more tracks of driving dance music.

"I Fall Down", opening with piano and evolving into a rolling rhythm, echoes the self-questioning of "Gloria", concerning one of the album's central themes, the struggle within yourself to remain good — a battle between good and evil that, fortunately , has wider interpretations than just Christian ones. "I Threw A Brick Through A Window" is the most immediately outstanding track, touching on funk, effectively using echo and hammered drums. Here the self-doubt in the song "No one is blinder than he who will not see/No one is blinder than me" is given the uplifting optimism of Bono's call to "Be my brother/There is another way out of here". The song has a passion both epic and personal, it is a call founded in a desperate wish to communicate.

"Rejoice" is the album's second theme. It does. "What am I to do/Just tell me what am I supposed to say/I can't change the world/But I can change the world in me/I rejoice!" The guitar and drums turn this into the most exciting anthem U-2 have come up with. Built on affirmation, it leaves the fearfulness of "Out of Control" firmly in the past.

The side closes with "Fire", the last single dealing again with a personal struggle, edged with optimism. And it is the contradiction in their positive attitude to the struggle that strikes such an emotional response in the listener. Side one is a powerful battle, but it is never depressing, nor shallowly uplifting.

Side two is less immediate. It advances the basic theme of the struggle to a more positive celebration of God, and in doing so forsakes the swift thrust of side one.

It opens with "Tomorrow", a musical adventure that will suprise you. Using haunting uileann pipes to provide a traditional Irish atmosphere, it unfolds a tale of family loss, a mixture of emigration and death, that eventually become a cry for Jesus, with U-2 powering in on top of the pipes. It is one of the most successful and impressive folk/rock combinations I have heard because it relies more on feeling and association than on purism.

"October", the title track, fills the place occupied on "Boy" by "The Ocean", and probably intentionally so. Once again it is a short song dealing evocatively with nature, but it moves from "The Ocean's" adolescent desire to change the world to U-2's more mature acceptance of their Christianity. The Edge plays a drifting piano while Bono sings sadly of shifting seasons, until he adds, "But you go on ... and on".

"With A Shout" is cartoon world U-2 — the album's weakest track, it is a shout of pain and joy that unfortunately sounds like U-2 playing a U-2 song with a badly written chorus. It exploits few of the tensions and dynamics in evidence elsewhere, and the use of a horn section seems purely technical rather than soul-felt.

"Stranger In A Strange Land" more than makes up for it, however. A complex, sad, powerful travelogue that catches the distance and strangeness of being alien to a place, grasping at the insights it gives you, It could be about the north of Ireland, America, England, emigration or simply the experience of being distanced by your own feelings. Bono's delivery of "I wish you were here/To see what I can see/To hear ... I wish you were here" is filled with poignancy. It is his perpetual call. It is what the album wants to achieve.

The final two songs are inarticulate in the most positive way. An optimism pervades both, which takes the emotions up. "Scarlet" says "rejoice" with a sleepy magic, while "Is That All" grows from the staccato guitar originally used in "The Cry" and asks, unbelieving, "Is

Adam chews on a plectrum. Pic: Colm Henry

that all you want from me?", a response to the offer in Gloria, "*If I had anything ... I'd give it to you*".

The album logically closes with tracks that lift you out of the emotional confusion U-2 charge into elsewhere. "October" ends in celebration.

Is that all? "October" is an LP of exciting, emotional, spiritually inclined rock: the most uplifting rock LP of the year, a modern dance that studies no trends, relies on no false aura of cool. It is a Christian LP that avoids all the pedantic puritanism associated with most Christian rock, avoids the old world emotional fascism of organised religion and the crusading preaching of someone like born-again Bob Dylan. It is fortunate that the main spiritual issues dealt with can be related to a wider frame of reference than Christianity: man's struggle to know and control himself and his own nature is something that comes to everyone in some guise. And its celebratory sound has the same positive touch as gospel music, it rejoices, and that feels good.

Well, *is* that all I want from U-2? No. U-2 can touch and involve as the best art should do, but I cannot relate to all their words because often they respond to the basic problems of life and youth with the catch-all of having a saviour. With a group like The Jam, I can respond with intellectual as well as emotional interest. I can only relate to what U-2 sing in a broad rather than specific sense.

But it *is* broad enough for me to become happily lost. U-2 are running with the wind, accelerating at the speed of life, breathing in an air of magic, shouting out. "*I can't change the world*", they sing, but they can and do add something to my world.

They rejoice. I celebrate. Passionate friends. ■

Neil McCormick
Vol 5 No. 20 October 16th, 1981

U-2 (Main Hall, RDS, Dublin)

The Kids

I WAS lost in the heart of a crowd, where recollections grow wild with fancy. Caught in a ... a ... landslide, a light show, a movement, a positive noise, a yee-haw, a whoopee cushion of gigantic proportions, and ...

Hello! Hello!

... a homecoming.

This was more than a gig, but it wasn't a party. It was the mutual celebration of an audience and a group. It was tribal in the way much rock can be but it had something more, a sense of community, which sent surges of anticipation and excitement through those present even before the group went on stage.

Four thousand people welcoming home U-2, four thousand and most of them younger than me (I'm only 20!). U-2 now belong to them, or rather with them. Because not only are they the only major Southern Irish success story since The Boomtown Rats, they are *young.* Young in the sense of being much the same age as their audience: they are our contemporaries, and more, still more, this youth is at the core of their identity; they take t and build it to epic proportions. It's not a matter of understanding their audience, there is no great insight nvolved here; it is that they are *part* of their audience, by birth, by sensibility, by commitment.

And so I can say this was a special occasion, but what *more* can I say? They were loud. They flash with a rock edge that has a rare beauty for these days. Bono breathes life, care and compassion in his exuberance, the Edge fills even a venue of these difficult proportions with the sound of guitar explorations, Adam makes mistakes and poses rock-awkwardly (but we forgive him for that). Larry is Larry and the light show is big and professional ... but the spirit of the occasion went beyond all that.

In some ways it was not so different from certain gigs in the past where we watched them grow (Resurrection hello), while in other ways it was sadly far removed from the intimate excitement of small gigs.

That's obvious, but U-2 have embraced their growth and their growing audience far more easily than most. With a shout. Shout it out.

Hello. Hello.

Neil McCormick
Vol 6 No. 2 January 8th, 1982

Bono celebrates at the RDS. Pic: Mark Classon.

Are Alright

U2 ~
Poll Winners Speak Out

Niall Stokes talks to Bono and The Edge about
their 1982 Hot Press Poll victory

With another sweeping Hot Press Readers' Poll victory under their collective belt, the inevitable conclusion is that the U-2 star is still unfalteringly in the ascendant. Their achievement in taking the overall Best Polling Act category, ahead of Elvis Costello and The Attractions, Altered Images, Human League and Paul Brady, as well as dominating the Irish section of the poll follows hard on an impressively improved showing in the NME poll, a highly successful sell-out Irish tour which took them up the scale to the 5,000-capacity RDS Main Hall in Dublin, and an equally celebratory brace of London gigs just prior to Christmas. It all adds up to a remarkable show of strength, carried all the more effectively because of the band's still-explosive sense of enthusiasm and commitment.

But while the band in building their audience, are making the kind of strides necessary to keep the enterprise creatively as well as financially buoyant, there have been some worrying developments over the past year. Even in this, the issue of Hot Press which celebrates a new and comprehensive triumph for the band, in terms of audience commitment, the letters page sees a hitherto unprecedented wave of disillusionment with them.

In a sense this is predictable – most bands find that achieving mass support means losing some of those who championed them through the early stages. But then U-2 have always been exceptional in their ability to break with the stereotypes. Their commitment is such that you feel they must want to transcend the inevitable, to find the key to the mystery of how not to alienate those who intially put their faith in the band, while attracting new support all the time.

On an entirely different level, there has been some disquiet following the band's lack of major singles success in Britain in 1981. Steering a tight course, the acceleration provided by a hit single can make the vital difference to ongoing record company commitment, or lack thereof. There is a need for record companies, to have some tangible verification of their belief in the commercial potential, even of bands signed essentially on the basis of musical credibility. Both "Fire" and "Gloria" looked set for lift-off but it didn't happen; executives at Island must have been perplexed, if not downright upset – all the more so because the company so obviously believes in the band.

How important these issues are is a matter for interpretation. Crucially, it depends on the attitude of the band. Anyone who knows U-2, anyone who's been touched by their music, anyone who's been fired by their magic should anticipate one thing: they are not complacent.

Currently back in the U.S of A., at the start of a strenuous six-week stint there, Bono is characteristically UP, when the poll news is delivered. "The sun is shining, The Edge is shining – we're all feeling very good", he says, reflecting on his exuberant torrent of words. "When I'm not feeling so good, I don't talk so fast".

But there is no sense, right now, of Bono being carried forward on a wave of undiluted optimism. Neither he nor his fellow U-2-ers are likely to shrink from the implications of their evolving status. And though their recent Irish tour and most specifically the Dublin RDS gig represented a pinnacle of achievement for them, they're quite prepared to question the scale

The Edge in Kilmainham Jail, 1982, where the band recorded their "Celebration" video. Pic: Colm He

which was involved.

"What we did was quite ambitious", the Edge says unassumingly about the RDS gig. "We haven't ever played a venue that size in our own right before. There was a feeling that maybe the occasion became larger than us — I think that it might have been better to play some small venues as well.

"But I'd still stand by those gigs", he adds, a theme taken up by Bono: "The concert in the RDS was the most successful concert ever of its size I've been at in Dublin. There was such an atmosphere of celebration, right from the front rows to the back. That kind of feeling between the band and the audience leaves me breathless".

There were aspects of the experience about which he feels apprehensive — the fact that some people were hurt for one, though it was, he emphasises, a peaceful concert. Then there was an incident in Cork, where a group of about fifty or sixty people came autograph-hunting.

"They didn't want to talk", he says and his voice registers bewilderment, "they wanted bits of me. They wanted me to write my name down on scraps of paper. Incidents like that did make me think about the whole thing — we're not into that gladiators, dinosaur rock thing.

"I'm asking a lot of questions about it but what I do believe is that the band is a great live act and we're going to continue to be a great live act".

Some of the disillusionment among "established" U-2 fans relates to the fact that a portion of their expanded audience responds to the band with imaginary-guitar poses — a tradition associated with the dinosaur bands U-2's vibrancy rejects. It's a spurious excuse for disaffection and Bono says as much.

"I don't look down on that", he asserts, "I don't care what people are, whether they've long hair, short hair or they're skinheads — if someone is being excited by the

78

music, then I'm happy. I don't care for cliches myself, or stock responses, but people get a chance to let go at our gigs and they do. As long as it's not violent or too alcoholic — and by that I don't mean being drunk, but becoming senseless — if people express themselves, then that's good. And if elitist followers are put off by that, then that's up to them.

"What I'd like to get across, without sounding trite, is that our belief in the people who come to see us is very strong. That's what's important about our relationship with our audience".

And what their success in Readers' Polls, and suchlike, generates is a feeling that "it's nice to have some of that belief back — we'd just like to say ... thank you!" And he sounds so wide-eyed that there's no way you could treat his guilelessness sceptically.

"I do feel that this is the end of a certain era", he adds seriously. "We are re-evaluating our position, both from a live and a recording point of view. We've just cancelled a planned tour of Australia, Japan and India because we want to spend more time at home.

"The band just loves Dublin and being there", he says outlining tentative plans which, if realised, might set the scene in their hometown alight.

The Edge is philosophical about the response to "October", which he describes as "very varied". "A lot of people who liked "Boy" were disappointed by it", he comments, "while people who didn't like "Boy" preferred "October". What the responses to the album indicate is that you can't come to terms with our music in one or two listens.

"I like it more now than I did at first", he adds, a feeling which is at odds with so many musicians' experience of their own work — the more they hear it, the more it grates. "It's like with "11 O'Clock" — that didn't get a great reaction when it was released but it came through two years or a year later to be voted Best Single on Dave Fanning's rock show. I think "October" will prove to be a very important album for the band".

Their new single, recorded a couple of weeks back in Dublin's fine Windmill Studios, he describes as a "short, sharp song".

"It's not a pop single as such", he adds, "but it is quite accessible. It's a single type of song, which is unusual for us — we've never really released a single as such — they've essentially been tracks from albums".

Hence their lack of smash hit singles is seen as basically irrelevant. In an era where most bands concentrate on singles, often to the detriment of their album output, U-2 see themselves as an album band.

"I've always thought of it in those terms", the Edge comments, "and Island have also. This is a long-term project. Even now they're delighted with progress — when we signed, they said that it might be the third album before things started happening" — a projection which can hardly be put down as overly optimistic, given their rate of progress so far.

"We never did want to be a band hoping for the next single to be a hit", he says, emphasising how easy it is to fall from grace in a fickle market. "Albums and live tours are our strength and the singles are essentially a promotional device for them".

On their evolving relationship with their audience he adds, "We aren't the sort of band you can make your mind up about and still be right in a year's time. It's more like a process of continual assessment. We're going to change and we're going to keep on changing. We're not restricting ourselves. But audiences are into that. Audiences are into progression".

If there is a theme in this short conversation, it's *that*

> **"What I'd like to get across, without sounding trite, is that our belief in the people who come to see us is very strong. That's what's important about our relationship with our audience." — *Bono***

faith — the credence which U-2 invest, some might say naively, in the quality of the ordinary people — the mass of ordinary people — who now form their audience. But in this attitude they are being entirely consistent. What has fired, and inspired their music from the word go, is an unshaking optimism, which flies in the face of so many signposts to the times, and which allows them to transcend even their own doubts, as well as the extraneous hostile forces which might have grounded their soaring vision.

What is important about this optimism is that it acts as a direct challenge to the essential bleakness imposed by those who offer youthful energy nothing more than the same old story. There is something to celebrate in the fact that where Irish youth lacked a voice for long, now there is not just one but many through which their cultural aspirations are being expressed.

U-2's power lies in their ability to capture musically the teeming rush of youthful experience. It's a power that won't be denied, that won't be perverted easily.

What those who feel that U-2 have gone too far up the ladder must remember is that they care passionately about keeping their achievement in perspective, that they are committed to its personal, human scale.

Our trust in them thus far has scarcely been misplaced. Now is not the time for faint hearts. ■

Niall Stokes
Vol 6 No. 5 February 19th, 1982.

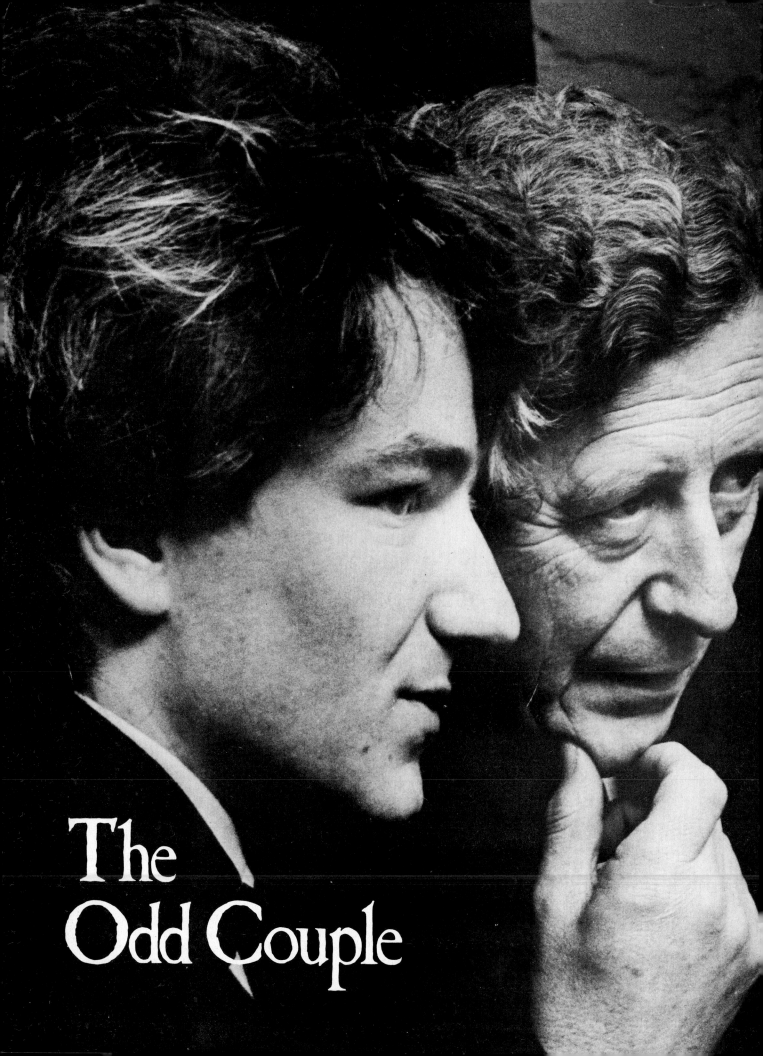

The Odd Couple

Bill Graham witnesses the summit meeting of U2 and Garret Fitzgerald.

JIMMY Carter settled on Bob Dylan as his favourite rock artist but Garret Fitzgerald's first rock preference is for The Byrd's "Turn Turn Turn".

The admission was extracted from the Fine Gael leader as he paid court to Bono and U-2 in Windmill Studios on the last Friday of the campaign. The transmutation of Garret The Good into Garret The Groover would have been familiar to Jimmy Carter, the first American presidential candidate to actively court the rock vote but it wasn't some scam dreamed up in Fine Gael headquarters. Basically, it was Bono's doing.

When in early summer, returning from a date in Finland, U-2 found themselves sharing the Heathrow departure lounge with Fitzgerald, Bono with typical audacity marched up to him and propelled himself into conversation. Then the two found themselves sharing the same row of seats on the flight to Dublin; Fitzgerald finally capitulated to one personality who can speak faster than him. After all, the pair do have similar religious interests.

By the time the plane landed Fitzgerald was almost offering Bono his Special Branch driver and car for a lift home to Howth and the two swopped addresses. It was only natural that Bono should give a fellow performer valuable publicity advice and invite Fitzgerald down for his most important photo session of the campaign with Colm Henry.

But seriously, the two had continued to correspond since that flying encounter. This unusual endorsement of Garret Fitzgerald stemmed from a real preference for the Fine Gael leader's personality over that of Bono's fellow Northsider, Charles J. Haughey. Charlie's showband associations may not have helped either.

The Sunday World had got wind of the story but U-2 didn't want it inserted in The Head's election round-up of entertainer's opinions. Nor did they want a party headquarters press conference celebrity rabbit-out-of-the-hat job. Mohammed had to come to the mountain, visit the studio and work for his endorsement.

It was a quiet day for Fitzgerald since he spent the afternoon studying the Book of Estimates in preparation for his debate with Haughey, so the 1.30 photo-call attracted the full gaggle of highly-confused national press correspondents to the one campaign story of the day. Then Garret Fitzgerald became the first senior Irish politician to sit at the mixing desk of a 24-track modern recording studio.

The camera-men snapped as Bono and The Edge explained the intricacies of recording to a somewhat perplexed and definitely impressed Fitzgerald and his wife, Joan. If the encounter achieved anything beyond its publicity value, its worth was in giving one establishment decision-maker an insight into the complexities of the recording business.

Certainly while the pair chatted as they posed for the photographers, Fitzgerald was learning the stamina required for touring as Bono outlined a typical European schedule. One young Irish businessman in a hi-tech industry was doing a useful lobbying job.

But the assembled hacks were more interested in one-liners. They got them when Bono displayed his characteristic nerve in inviting the Fitzgeralds to dinner with himself and his newly-wed Alison, when Fitzgerald joked about his own lousy singing in the bath and when Bono quipped about being Tanaiste.

Since Fianna Fail previously have received the support of The Fureys and The Chieftains, U-2's action doesn't set a completely new precedent. But as they made clear, this was a personal endorsement for Fitzgerald the man, not a clause-by-clause acceptance of the Fine Gael manifesto. Nor, as one report mistakenly had it, was or is Bono a member of Young Fine Gael.

Also with pirate radio stations assiduously courting politicians, rock as an industry may have suffered from its shyness in fighting for its interests. I suspect Bono, U-2 and their manager Paul McGuinness figured Garret Fitzgerald could prove more useful than a helping hand!

In the transparent nature of these affairs, Garret didn't really hear the new album. But I *did* and enough to calm any fears that U-2 are going respectable. If anything "War" takes a reverse direction.

It certainly isn't Son of Son of "Boy". When most groups have spent '82 brightening their sound, U-2 wager that 1983 will be the year of the guitar and they've opted for a much more grating, dirtier sound from The Edge while Adam and Larry's rhythm contributions give the band a more pronounced modern New York r 'n' b feel.

Whereas their two previous albums had a pastoral daylight mood, "War" takes U-2's music into the fearful big city night. If "Blade Runner" had been filmed around the inner city, "War" would have made its perfect soundtrack and that's not something you could say about their previous work.

When Garret Fitzgerald left, the band and Steve Lillywhite got back to work with two songs still requiring vocal tracks and their final mix. The Once And Future Taoiseach now has his professional responsibilities. So do U-2.■

Bill Graham
Vol 6 No. 20, December 3rd, 1982

Bono with Garret Fitzgerald. Pic: Colm Henry

Blood on the Tracks

Liam Mackey reviews "War"

THE ARMAGEDDON Time is definitely upon us, the evidence darkening doorsteps and television screens in Beirut, Belfast, London, Washington, El Salvador, Afghanistan, Dublin, Moscow, Baghdad, Teheran, Warsaw, Port Stanley — there can be few places on this small planet which remain untouched, either directly or indirectly, by the Plague.

In this flickering light peace can appear to be a temporary condition, an aberration, a simple twist of fate — here today, gone tomorrow. In the 1980's the new, officially-approved symbol of peace shows the earth bisected by two nuclear missiles, nose to nose — to be capable of the ultimate destruction is to rest easy in your bed tonight.

It's against this blood-soaked backdrop that U-2 release their third album, a record which bears witness to its time and context with a mixture of fear, courage and hope. In the face of prejudice and deep-rooted embitterment, whose physical language is expressed in the bomb and the gun, this record waves a white flag, not of toothless surrender, but of sanity.

The cynical may scoff and deem the act a useless, even fatuous, exercise, but the cynical are already doomed, having prematurely pronounced the death sentence on themselves. Agreed, no one can claim, as in daze of yore, that rock 'n' roll music is going to change the world — to believe that is to fall into the same trap that caught the most passionate and well-intentioned of the celebrated sixties' idealists. But to accept that nothing can be said or done, is to be even more culpable. Obviously, we all need our palliatives, which is why people as diverse as Duran Duran and The Dynatones gain credence and currency in different hearts and charts, but the fact remains that rock 'n' roll, because of its universal popularity with the generation which is in the best — if not, indeed, the only — position to do something to help cure the disease, can be a vital force.

U-2 are aware enough to know this to be true, intelligent enough to know that to pretend to have all the answers would be false. "*I don't know which side I'm on/I don't know my right from left/or my right from wrong*" sings Bono on "Two Hearts Beat As One", but it's clear he's certain that two hearts *are* better than one — and that, we must all concede, is the only starting point from which anything productive is likely to ensue.

U-2's "War" may be important because it raises real-life issues which all too many of the band's contemporaries choose, for various reasons, to ignore, but it's also vital in terms of the band's own development. As such it is a major leap forward, conceptually and technically, quickly persuading this listener to the view that it totally eclipses their previous two albums. I'll even go a step further and proclaim "War", among the major albums of the last few years and, in the Irish context, the most stunning and completely realised set since the Radiators' heinously ignored "Ghostown".

Indeed, there are a couple of tracks here which broach subjects and ideas that were also tackled in The Radiators' epic set. "Sunday Bloody Sunday", the opening track, is a title with a particularly acute resonance for people living on this island. It's obviously an emotive subject, the events of the two days which have equal claim to the title being amongst the most cold-blooded and tragic in our history. Principally because of that, the Bloody Sundays of Croke Park and Derry, have come to serve as further ammunition for those who feel that the retaliation must continue, the fighting must go on, resulting in an endless saga of eye-for-an-eye and tooth-for-a-tooth mutual tragedy.

U-2's "Sunday Bloody Sunday" takes the widescreen view, as over a powerful riff and machine-gun drumming, criss-crossed by skipping violin, Bono cries: "*And the battle's just begun/There's many lost but tell me who has won/The trenches dug deep within our hearts/Our Mother's children, brothers sisters torn apart*".

The message that hearts have been hardened, that battlelines drawn so many years before are being manned anew by successive generations is punched home in "Like A Song": "*Too set in our ways to re-arrange, too right in our wrong in this rebel song*", In other words, nothing but the same old story.

"The Refugee" on top of side two is a song which personalises the effects of war, sketching in a few vivid lines the sad plight of a young girl who watches as her father goes off to fight "*but he doesn't know what for*". The soundtrack is awesome, Bono's vocal a stuttering rage over a visceral, African-influenced, sonic storm — a radical departure for the band.

Indeed U-2 break moulds right throughout this

album. Much has been made of '83 being the year in which the guitar supposedly fights back, but it's unlikely that many will deploy the instrument with the resourcefulness and imagination demonstrated by The Edge on tracks like "New Year's Day" and "Red Light". Whether utilising electric or — as in the excellent anti-nuclear song "Seconds" and elsewhere on this album — acoustic guitar, The Edge's contribution is crucial to the shaping of U-2's startling new music.

There are influences of course — definitively urban New York funk informs the pulsing "Two Hearts Beat As One" for example — but ultimately U-2's debts are utterly subservient to their own unique musical vision. If confirmation were needed, "War" offers watertight evidence of the band's standing as a genuinely original

force in contemporary music.

Despite reviewing this album under less than optimum circumstances (it's a cassette copy bereft of information and there's a deadline hanging over my head — send flowers and messages of sympathy to this address, etc.), I'm still convinced that in "War", U-2 have fashioned an album of major import. And knowing from experience that U-2 records get better with repeated listenings, I can only urge you, regardless of your opinion on the band to date, to take a listen to this album.

For my money, this is a flag truly worth rallying around, this is the beat surrender to succumb to.■

Liam Mackey
Vol 7 No. 3 February 18th, 1983.

The People's Choice

U2 hit No. 1 in Britain. Bill Graham reports

Pic: Anton Corbijn.

Driving into Heathrow Airport six weeks ago, Island Press Officer Neil Storey played me an advance tape of U-2's "War" Album. "It's going to be a Number 1 album", he predicted boldly, reflecting a feeling which was building momentum within the Island organisation.

I demurred. "War" was definitely destined to be U-2's biggest-selling album yet in the U.K., a certain top ten entrant and a probability for the top five — but predicting it to climb above all other competition seemed too brave, too optimistic a tip.

So much for the supposed advantages of journalistic detachment and objectivity. Overnighting in Bristol, U-2 woke up on Tuesday morning to find that "War" had performed the rare feat of entering the British album charts at No. 1 — the ultimate public accolade for their far-sighted fortitude in organising their affairs their own way. While the trend-sighters had been swivelling around looking for the new movement to start the year, boosted by the crucial success of their "New Year's Day" single, U-2 had slipped through their intelligence nets to land the ultimate prize.

No television sets were hurled from their hotel bedroom. U-2 don't celebrate that way. Speaking last Sunday from London, Bono admitted to a champagne breakfast, quaffed from the bottles sent by well-wishers but the morning's main business had been "to excavate Adam from his bed and throw him in the shower" — the blonde bass-player having been partying well if not wisely till 8 in the morning.

By Bono's account, it was the roadcrew, the "Cork Mafia" of Joe O'Herlihy and Tom Mullally and Dubliner Steve Iredale who were the most demonstrative. "You know those white flags we have at the back of the stage", he recounted, "well we really had to stop them bringing out the tricolour!..."

85

Nonetheless, the success of "War" must have suprised those who thought U-2 had vanished. It was a false impression, based on the simplistic belief that all creative and commercial activity is suspended once an act is off the front-covers. In fact — and this now makes absolute and indisputable sense — U-2's policy of strategic withdrawal through '82 was both intentional and well-founded.

Having toured exhaustively — and exhaustingly — through Britain, Europe and America, U-2 knew they had made hostage a fiercely loyal audience, certain to immediately support their next album. They also knew that they couldn't sustain the pressure of such touring schedules.

Personally, all four members needed a respite. Otherwise as they grew from "Boy" to men, all their earlier friendships might have been sundered by their global expeditions. Bono's wedding was but the public expression of the need to recover their private lives back in Dublin.

They were also aware that this, their third album, had to be conceived without distraction; the experience of "October" couldn't be repeated. Though a more sustantial album than its critics admit, "October" essentially was prepared in pressured studio sessions, hurried on by fast-approaching release deadlines.

"October" certainly had a solid basis in both the band's own early ideas and those discovered in the first

> ## "Sometimes I'm actually getting fed up with being 'Bono'. It's a group that's made good. I can see people going down to buy a newspaper and saying 'it's not that guy on the cover yet again'".

thrill of touring outside Ireland. For their third album, they had to start uniquely from scratch. Further touring, besides the few European festival dates they accepted, would have scuppered creativity at source.

They also knew the breed of album they wanted. When all around were cleansing their sound, U-2 refused studio disinfectants. "War" is a slap in the face" says Bono. "We wanted an album that would separate us from our contemporaries".

Even as far back as the recording of "October", Bono was speaking of his own demand for a harsher texture, an album with a more genuine noisome and aggressive style than the sparkling, quicksilver sound they seemed to be framing.

They weren't certain that their long-standing cohort

Steve Lillywhite, producer of both "Boy" and "October", would continue working with them. The reasons weren't down to a rift in common purpose. Rather, Lillywhite has his own self-imposed rule that he doesn't work on more than two albums with any one act since he believes the relationship inevitably becomes stale on later collaborations. U-2 also felt it might be beneficial to move on.

But when other name producers were checked out on preliminary sessions, none met the exacting demands they make on any potential fifth creative contributor. Last summer I remember Bono speaking disappointedly of one international luminary whom they found to be essentially an engineer and a personality insufficiently assertive to stand up to them. "We were walking all over him" said Bono, or words to that effect …

They just couldn't find the individual with the right stuff to lead them through to their vision of the new U-2 sound. After that unrequited quest, Lillywhite's entry was re-assured.

But the innovations on "War" aren't limited to the instrumental sound; the advances in using the Edge's voice are a second factor in changing the U-2 texture.

"He's got a really under-rated voice" Bono reminds me. "After all his father is a member of the Dublin Welsh Male Voice Choir. It's his voice, not mine, that we double-track for harmonies. It's also him who comes in on the chorus singing "Sunday Bloody Sunday".

Edge also has his own showcase on "Seconds", which establishes his credibility in this respect, unequivocally.

Bono also argues that his own singing has developed. "If you listen to "Red Light", there's this blues thing like "Twist And Shout" when I'm singing "Alone in the Spotlight", he says. But his most abiding memory is of Steve Lillywhite "making me sing 'till I bled".

Other fond personal memories are of his wife Alison's support when he was fighting a mental block about his lyrics, particularly on "Sunday Bloody Sunday". "She was kicking me out of the bed in the morning. She literally put the pen in my hand".

And when he adds that "Surrender" has multiple meanings once one "goes beneath the top soil", the reference is clear.

There was much to savour in January's "Top of The Pops" watching U-2, Echo and the Bunnymen and Wah! all scale the charts, the critics ' class of '80, later fickly discounted by the more fashion-conscious among the press gang. It had been forgotten by those who abandoned the good ship, that bunnyrabbits and other creatures of the same breed are prone to hibernation.

Certainly there had been no doubts within the U-2 camp about the band's resolution — those with access to

Pic: Colm Henry

it were convinced all along that "War" would be a major album. Even if this witness retained some scepticism about the likelihood of it arriving directly at Number 1, I had heard enough to realise that it was the genuine article, the epic album they had always been threatening to make. It was also common knowledge that Island would give it unremitting support in the belief that U-2 had built an unfailingly devoted audience, increased to potential major league status by the new fans who had come to the group through "New Year's Day".

"It could be our "Tropical Gangsters" of next year", Island Publicity Director Rob Partridge told Niall Stokes back in December — the phenomenal sales of that album indicating just how big U-2's record company were thinking.

Their British tour selling out before it began confirmed the band's chances. Says Bono of their bolstered audience: "You knew something was happening when people were trekking overnight across Britain and sleeping in the back of buses, coming from Bristol, Liverpool, even Holland!".

Inevitably in Bono's words, last week it got "Silly". The anecdotes unfold. After Bristol they journeyed to Exeter and "well, you know us, we have this running battle with champagne", Bono states. They didn't get sprayed on stage — the cork refused to pop!

In Cardiff on Saturday, Bono (wisely) didn't give his opinions on the Arms Park Rout or (unwisely!) on Bonnie Tyler's video. Instead "with the Edge's Welsh heritage, I got the audience to sing "Land of My Fathers" and the 3,000 of them burst into song".

Poole found Island hiring a bus for the company's works celebration outing, an emotional event for their London office whose recent successes have come from New York and Jamaican signings, rather than what's been developed from their own doorstep. This Sunday, Bono has the time to credit Island's version of the soft-sell. "People always tend to think of people working in a record company as cogs in an evil machine but we've always found the people in Island excellent and helpful to work with", he says.

Plaudits which go to the press office will be confirmed by Hot Press — but there's now a new dimension to be managed by them, as Fleet St. targets in. "There's been a lot of people booking into hotels" insinuates Bono.

He's definitely disinterested in their advances, wary of the warped celebrity that might be on offer: "I refuse the pressure, I don't acknowledge it".

Indeed, worried about overkill, Bono's also thinking of taking himself off public display to allow his fellows come further forward into the spotlight. At the start of our phone-call, he confesses, "Sometimes, I'm actually getting fed up with being Bono" — and you can hear the quotation marks — "It's a group that's made good. I can see people going down to buy a newspaper and saying "it's not that guy on the cover, yet again".

English and Irish newspapers might be wise to expect a slackening of the verbal salvos from his direction.

Nevertheless, while Bono's still bubbling, some further choice anecdotes. Like the one about the back-handed compliment from the black security guard after their Cardiff date: "He was six foot by six and he said he didn't understand why we were a success. He watched just about everybody passing through that dressing room and he said they all assumed a role, they all changed their clothes and their minds from being on and off stage. Whereas we didn't, we were the same people both on and off stage".

Even if he's still leery of fashion, he's alert enough to recognise the rise of groups like Southern Death Cult and the Sex Gang Children and note the badges of the fans who foregather in their dressing room. Having checked out such bands live, his opinion is that U-2's breakthrough "is endorsed by the rise of those bands".

But any such associations are an extra. Bono's proudest boast is that "we're not a Wave. We're not part of anything, we're part of ourselves. Now we know we're on our own and I'm so glad".

What next? Obviously America beckons: U-2 move on over for a two-month tour there, beginning mid-April. Released simultaneously with Britain, "War" is already enlarging their audience in the States too. Radio stations previously resistant to U-2 are adding it to their playlists, the album having registered as the "Most Added" album of last week on the three influential business Tip sheets. Against that optimistic backdrop, a healthy 200,000 copies have already been shipped in its first ten days on release. With "War" already in the top 20 in Scandinavia and the Low Countries, U-2 are moving up and out.

"Two Hearts Beat As One" is the next single, to be released with a free disc which will feature a remix of both it and "New Year's Day" by New York disco-mix ace Francis Kevorkian. The same Kevorkian has further plans for the Edge. Slated to produce Island's latest signing, Jah Wobble, he hopes to lure the guitarist into sessions for the album.

Other extra-curricular activities are planned: while the magnificent success of "War" must sweep them along in its tide, it won't blind them to other possibilities.

So the wind blows. U-2's dramatic emergence should only surprise those who haven't followed their career, who've not noted the qualities of care, determination, nerve and obvious talent by which they've shaped their career. Live, Bono can seem foolhardy but U2 have never run a ship of fools.

Actually, Philip Lynott may have pronounced one fundamental reason for their breakthrough: In an earlier *Hot Press* interview, his trouper's standards led him to complain that, despite the undoubted studio and attitudinal achievements of the new bands, few if any had shown the same capacity to generate the same peak experiences and live excitement once they quit the clubs for the larger halls. U-2's arrival is partly due to British audiences belatedly realising the point of that criticism: U-2 have worked assiduously on generating that grass roots support in a manner reminiscent of our other career stars, Thin Lizzy and Rory Gallagher. They never shirked hard graft, the punishing grind of extensive

Pic: Anton Corbijn.

touring that builds fans' loyalties even in obscure places. Now that commitment is being returned to them.

Patently some must ask: will success spoil U-2? Certainly not, if the fear is that they'll be contracting the most viciously insulating social disease of celebrity. The crucial test, the real initiation for U2, occurred when they were escaping from Ireland to their international contract and proving their worth to their first world audiences. Ego-corrupting influences would have taken hold then, if they were going to ... First time out of Ireland, going to L.A. receptions, you learn the basics of self-protection.

Anyway Bono's on the phone stating the truth that "there's an awfully big rift between being number 1 and number 2. Beating Michael Jackson — it couldn't happen to a nicer guy".

Actually, that's not a back-hander, he does admire the thriller but given the agenda, we weren't stopping to swop opinions on Michael Jackson. Still I'll take the liberty and get pushy with my ideal ...

Number One in Britain is fine but swopping guest appearances with M.J. is when it really counts! ■

Bill Graham

Vol 7 No. 5, March 18th, 1983

CITY built on hills, surrounded by snow-capped mountain ranges, lakes & the Pacific Ocean; blazing sunshine all day long, lying in a park with a cold "Bud" in one hand, just people watching: roller skaters, skateboarders, joggers, windsurfers, canoeists and sail-boats on the lake – everyone's smiling, tapes blaring out from portable stereos or walkmans, boogying along at a leisurely pace.

In the evenings the bars fill up, one place even has great draught Guinness! Paradise, but Seattle just needs that little injection of the fast life, to liven things up a bit, and last night it certainly got it!

U-2 have hit the U.S. in a way nobody could have foreseen. After about 25 dates in one month the show has been polished to virtual perfection, reaching a high I haven't seen in a live performance for a long time. Every date has been a sell-out: venues have ranged in size from 2,000 to 12,000 seaters and everywhere the story has been the same – crowd reactions comparable in emotion only to Springsteen at Wembley.

But before you think this is yet another U-2 fanatic who never said a bad word about the band, let me make my position clear. I've seen U-2 fairly regularly since the Buttery days along with D.C. Nien; those smaller gigs were great but since then I haven't seen a U-2 gig that could be described as classic: I've seen average shows, promising shows, but nothing spectacular. I possess only one U-2 album, and a couple of singles. I follow them with interest and hope as I follow any Irish band – but that's the size of it.

Tonight's venue was similar in style to the Olympia theatre in Dublin, with seats and a capacity of just under 3,000; my first reaction was that it wouldn't work but after about three songs, seats were the last thing on anyone's mind – the place just literally shook with excitement, inspired by Adam and Larry's thudding bass and drums, The Edge's harmonics responding to every signal from Bono – the band were giving absolutely everything they had. At this stage, halfway through the tour, they should be exhausted, cutting corners and playing songs as a matter of form rather than feeling, but not a chance; every note, every beat had a sense of vibrancy and commitment. They pranced around the stage as if it was only their second night on the road.

About halfway through the set Bono used the familiar introduction "This song is not a rebel song" and the band lurched into "Sunday Bloody Sunday" – the response at the end was thunderous. Then into "New Year's Day" probably their best known song on this side of the Atlantic, and the reaction again was unbelievable.

Bono added a few deft touches to make a "show" of it, first giving one of the by now familiar white flags into the audience; it was duly passed up to the people on the balcony, to the back of the hall, and back up to the stage again. At another point Bono stopped everything and mentioned that someone had been ringing him in his hotel all afternoon, claiming to be from Seattle's greatest band – was this guy in the audience? It turned out he was and Bono invited him onto the stage; he was the drummer so some extra drums were brought on stage, and one extremely happy Seattleite played percussion for a couple of songs. Later Bono disappeared from the stage and suddenly reappeared in the centre of the crowd, microphone in hand, and continued singing there; he was lifted up by the crowd and lying on his back carefully passed back up to the stage. At the end of the show during an encore, he asked a girl up from the audience and they performed Bono's version of a "jig". He then sat her at the front of the stage, borrowed her friend's camera and proceeded to take a few shots of her.

Each one of these acts turned the audience to virtual hysteria: Americans love participation and they love a performer.

Closing the show with "I Will Follow" and "Gloria", U-2 left an audience which was now riding in overdrive; the first encore was one I hadn't heard before, a quiet ballad, with the Edge playing a semi-acoustic. They bounced back with "Two Hearts Beat As One" leaving an audience still screaming for more – and finished with another slower number, the Edge playing bass and Adam on guitar. The band left the stage one by one, Larry filing off last with the sound of his snare drum still pounding through the P.A. and the crowd still roaring. A tape of Clannad's "Theme From Harry's Game" followed by Stockton's Wing meant the end of the show and a dripping, exuberant crowd quietly weaved their way back onto the streets.

Seattle will not forget them for a long, long time!

Cecil Hollwey
Vol 7 No. 12 June 24th, 1983.

Articulate Speech of the Heart

Bono interviewed by Liam Mackey

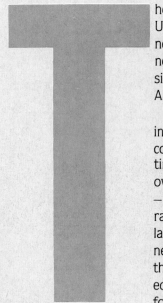

The following interview with U-2's Bono took place in the neat bungalow on the beach near Howth which the singer shares with his wife Alison.

Unlike so many rock interviews which are conducted under very strict time limitations — Bono's own record is 16 in one day! — this was a long and free-ranging conversation which lasted from midnight until near dawn and yielded up three full hours of tape, the equivalent of 60 pages of foolscap transcript. Present for the initial part of the conversation were Bono, Alison, yours truly and my partner in crime Rosemarie but the bulk of the interview was a one to one exchange — with the notable exception of an odd and somewhat disquieting incident on the road near the house around four in the morning. As we were walking and talking a car pulled up at the kerb beside us, out of which popped a Henry Cooper lookalike — either a cop or a vigilante; when asked he refused to identify himself and since he was fondling a wrench in his right hand, we didn't exactly push the point — who gave us a snappy interrogation before climbing back into his car and speeding off into the night. But that, as they say is another story. And if *this* story is to get to press on time, we'd best dispense with all other formalities and get straight down to business.

As you join us, cheese crackers and coffee are being consumed, Bono is vaulting through the years and, in defiance of the laws of mathematics, explaining how four into one can go. It was music, he says, which forged their friendship rather than vice versa.

"We were four completely different people, four people going nowhere and we decided to go there together. Four rejects, on all different levels, from the system. Four people — four intelligent people — who probably wouldn't be accepted for the E.S.B. or The Civil Service. The only thing we had in common was the music but there was, and is, quite an odd unity.

"We go to parties all the time", he says jumping back to the present, "be it L.A., New York, London, wherever, people throw parties for us and everybody arrives — tennis stars, people in the movie business. They're all there. And four of us will go into this room, rapping away to different people and you'll find an hour later, the same four people all talking to each other. And yet we've been on a bus together or in a hotel room all day long. And to this day, there is no friction".

And the cast, as it was in the beginning ...

"There was Edge and his brother Dik — two people who were anti-guitar heroes, anti-heroes full stop. Edge would only take his guitar out on formal occasions — not a man to sleep with it. Or even put new strings on it!

"And there was Adam who was the guy who would wear a dress into school or take his clothes off when we were rehearsing. He was always into vibing people out. Into blowing heads.

"And there was Larry. It's Larry's fault — he *did* start it. He's a very complex character. The way he hits the bass drum is the thing that makes this group still a rock 'n' roll group (as well as all the other things). People talk about U-2 being a "live group" or "the only live group" and they'll talk about me as the singer; because Bono will jump off the balcony to make a point — but it's not me at all, it's Larry's bass drum".

And Bono, self-confessed "introvert and extrovert"; please allow him to introduce himself.

"That's another thing. I'm the singer in the group U-2 and people expect things from me that I can't quite honestly give them — which is to be the life and soul of the party. There are nights when I'll stand up on the table and I'll take my clothes off (*laughs*) and there'll be another night when I'm afraid to even sit down ..."

"... or walk into a room", says Alison.

Bono: "It's something for Ali to understand — there

are nights when I'll be petrified about things. In school it was the same.

"Right now, when we've just come back from the American tour — and I've been used to being on-stage every night — round about 9 o'clock I start rocking in the chair and there's something trying to get out of me. But that's something I share with my father — containing within me these total opposites. If people think of me as "The Lad", they're making a big mistake — they've got it very wrong.

"When I'm talking to you, I'm talking to a lot of people who are interested in what I'm interested in which is music — and our music. So I'm talking to an audience as well as to you and I open myself up to you because I'm opening myself up to my audience.

"So sometimes when I meet a writer it was "No bullshit! Wham! There it is!" and a lot of people fell backwards. And sometimes it would come out as: "with some groups" — and I remember this — "With some groups you have to really fight hard to find out what they have on their mind but with Bono he's giving it to you" and it's all "what a nice guy" and sometimes I want to say "look, I'm *not* a nice guy — shut up — I'll slap your face — I'll show you that you're misunderstanding what I'm trying to do." 'Cos I know what I'm doing. I'm not stupid. But I'm not prepared to go through the bullshit and I think that's important to understand".

U-2's road to Damascus experience — the event which transformed them from being what Bono describes as "the world's worst garage band" into a group which could, and would evolve into a major force on the international stage — was that first memorable realisation of their own creative potential.

"That was an amazing feeling," says Bono. "Creativity! There is nothing there, it's a vacuum, a void and suddenly there is something there and it's a song and it says something — maybe significant, maybe insignificant. And it can be played on radios all over the world from Tokyo to San Francisco. That's the potential of a song and it's an amazing potential. And when we started watching songs come out, our own songs that sounded like nobody else — *that* was exciting".

The creative process still fascinates Bono. He gets up from his chair and rewinds a tape in a ghettoblaster — a present he got which is so enormous that a person would require the shoulder padding of an American pro-footballer to carry it in the *de rigeur* fashion — zeroing in at the beginning of the first of three songs he'll play during the course of the night. Actually, the word "song" is somewhat misleading. In reality the music, recorded live at soundchecks, is in a very embryonic state, but as

the various instruments, at first tentatively and then with increasing assurance fall into place and develop the theme, one can catch the spark of U-2's special alchemy. Bono provides an enthusiastic running commentary, pointing out that not a note I'm hearing had been rehearsed prior to recording. It's the sound of flesh and blood being applied to the merest ghost of an idea.

"That's four people who really know each other" he says with justifiable pride. "That's what comes of being a group. There are very few *groups* in the world really. There are a lot of groups with a singer or something but it's not the same."

Bono fast forwards the tape and locates another sketch captured at a soundcheck in Florida. Heard in its nascent, formative stage this music has a haunting appeal, The Edge's guitar clear and singing. Bono reveals that the guitarist has recently been listening to "a lot of Nigerian guitar players, also Ry Cooder, people like that".

And even as I'm listening to a song evolving on tape, U-2's music, in the broader sense, continues to evolve — because if it's to retain its vitality it has to.

"You can't parody yourself", Bono states. "There were so many groups sounding like us at one point that when we'd play a song we'd say "that sounds a bit like U-2 — hold on a second we *are* U-2!" (*laughs*) — that was happening. You nearly parody yourself and you've got to stop. That was what Edge had to do anyway.

"People all over America say "what about these people who are robbing your sound!" and Edge's reply to that has always been, "well look, y'know fine, take the sound — but it's not a sound that makes music good, it's where that sound comes and why it's coming out of a person and they can't copy that.

"And it is definitely The Edge. The crew have a joke about it. They have to set up his amps and put the guitar on and I've put my fingers where Edge puts his fingers and I've had his amps and his machines and the settings that he has them on and I've played and it sounds like ... no good! And it's *him* it's truly the way he plays and I think whatever instrument he plays will always have that distinctive quality. But there was a time when he was so distinctive he was running into trouble. So he stopped playing it and got into rock 'n' roll guitar and he got into acoustic guitar".

When Bono says that "everyone has their own theory about this group — what it is we really are", he's scarcely being self-indulgent. For a band who have so openly and honestly expressed themselves from the outset, U-2 have, paradoxically, had to deal with an inordinate amount of misinterpretation and even prejudice. At the very least, there have been a lot of misconceptions. Bono catalogues a few of them.

"First of all we started out and made "Boy" which is a sexual L.P. and we changed the cover in America to stop any concern there might be about paedophilia and the like because it was our first album. But import copies got in and, as you know, in America a lot of music is broken first in gay clubs and so we had a gay audience, a lot of people who were convinced the music was specifically for them. So there was a misconception if you like.

"Then in London there was the whole conception of "Paddies" maybe. "What are they?" They thought of the Boomtown Rats, they thought of Rory Gallagher, they though of Van the Man — "Irishness" was even a box people tried to put us into but that's a box we're quite proud to be in because our music *is* Irish.

"Then after "Boy" we made "October" which is a spiritual elpee and a lot of people went: "What the hell is going on here" — especially in England where people wouldn't be aware of how much religion is part of everyday life here in Ireland and how much stick people get here. They're not aware of how deep that runs. So they went off on that one for a while.

"So then "War" came out and to some people in America again, it was "the political band" and they loved it and they failed to see that "War" was an emotional elpee rather than a political one.

"So there have been misconceptions all the way and it's like chasing your tail. So I just stopped. But I find it interesting to see the amount of controversy that surrounds a group, I mean, I have heard amazing stories, about myself that I only wish were true. (*laughs*)".

Still, the myths persist. Earlier, on the day I talked with Bono, an acquaintance upon learning that I was going to do a U-2 interview announced that the group were his "pet hate" describing them scornfully as "goody goody Christians" or words to that effect. It's not the first time that Bono has heard such blanket allegations.

"That arose because journalists failed to see the intelligence of what we were doing in avoiding those rock 'n' roll games", he retorts. "A lot of people talked about trying to avoid cliches in their music but they weren't interested in trying to avoid cliches in their lifestyle.

"It was like "Boy" — the child's face. 'Is this about innocence — Oh, they're innocent' That's the joke. We were trying to do what a lot of those people in papers were talking about but when it hit them, they didn't realise what it was. As Edge says: "We beat them at our own game". We knew what we were doing.

"People talk about taboos in rock 'n' roll. People say

Bono with Bruce Springsteen

that "they're into breaking down taboos", like say, S & M or whatever. They talk about all this and it's totally *conservative.* They talk about music and how it should open up to new areas. Look, there are few singers, few musicians, few painters who aren't aware of the third part of their being — the spirit. And I just expressed that in the music and a few people pressed the panic button.

"But I was determined. And getting back to John Lennon (whose music Bono has been listening to recently) *there* was a man who, however unfashionable however uncontemporary his beliefs were, *because* they were his beliefs, he exposed himself. He was saying, well this is it, what do you want — no music or the truth? Because if I lie, the music will choke on itself. That's the choice. And I was going through that on "October" — what is the choice, write about Johnny and Mary or what? Would you like me to ram love songs down your throat, love songs that I don't believe in? People used to say that U-2 have never written love songs — well what do they want instead of that? I mean do people prefer lies? I think that's the question people should ask.

"As it is the lyrics are autobiographical — and there are four people in this group not one. Our music is not just inviting people to my own nightmare or daydream. It's much more than that. It is, when it comes down to it, very aggressive rock 'n' roll music — very aggressive. I think it's aggressive in its insight as well as in the music. And I think you feel you're doing something right when you get plus and minus reaction like we've been getting.

"People would not react if I went out and carried on like Elvis Presley or Mick Jagger or David Bowie. People *do* react if I go out and carry on like Bono. And I like that.

"I'm not a religious person. I'm frightened by religion. I've seen what it's done to this country. I've seen what it's done to people around me ... I've never allowed anybody to ram anything down *my* throat and I would never try to do the same thing."

That's the best indication that I'm right for my time".

And, one more time with feeling. Bono makes it clear that his faith, based on his own personal beliefs and values, has nothing to do with the rabid proselytising of the Born-again movement nor the dogmaticism of traditional organised religion.

"I'm not a religious person", he states emphatically. "I'm frightened by religion. I've seen what it's done to this country. I've seen what it's done to people around me. I go to America and I turn on my television set and I start sweating profusely because those guys have turned faith into an industry. It's appalling. It's ugly — this guy's hand is virtually coming out of the television set and I just want to throw the television out the window. I'm not a guy who went to mass every week. I've never allowed anybody to ram anything down *my* throat and I would never try to do the same thing".

We move on to talk about "War", U-2's third album and the one which through its outstanding commercial successes in Britain and America, confirmed the band's arrival as an international force. Creatively, it was no less important, the music showing U-2's determination to expand the frontiers of their sound while lyrically, it saw them moving on from the essentially introspective writing they'd concentrated on in the past, to tackle wider issues of the day.

As Bono puts it: "Whereas the previous two elpees had been inward-looking, "War" was outward looking. Whereas the previous two elpees had, in the lyric sense, been impressionistic, splashing paint on the canvas, "War" was more like graffiti, I suppose."

"Sunday Bloody Sunday" was the song, which especially in Ireland, aroused most interest, but it was the band's experience of Irish-American republican sentiment on their U.S. tour which directly influenced its creation. Bono recalls one particular incident which stopped him in his tracks.

"I walked out of the backstage door in San Francisco and there were about 30 or 40 people waiting for a chat and for autographs and I was scrawling my name on bits of paper as they were handed to me. I got this one piece of paper and was about to write on it and something in me said "hold on a second". The paper was folded and when I opened it, there was this big dogma thing looking for signatures — I was about to sign my name on a petition to support some guy I'd never heard of, an Irish guy with republican connections. And I got worried at that stage.

"I mean as much as I'm a republican I'm not a very territorial person. The whole idea of the white flag on stage was to get away from Green White and Orange, to get away from the Stars and Stripes, to get away from the Union Jack. I am an Irishman and we are an Irish group — stop! But I'm frightened of borders, frightened of restrictions on those levels and I get scared when people start saying they're prepared to kill to back up their belief in where a border should be. I mean, I'd love to see a united Ireland but I just don't believe you can put a gun to somebody's head, at anytime to make him see your way.

"Sunday Bloody Sunday" is a day that no Irishman can forget but *should* forget which is what we were saying – "how long must we sing this song?" When I introduce it I say: "this isn't a rebel song". The name comes up all the time and we're saying "how long must we have songs *called* "Sunday Bloody Sunday". That's one area in which I agree with Bob Geldof – history is just one mistake after another".

I suggest that perhaps the North of Ireland's greatest tragedy is the conditioning which sees each new generation (with honourable exceptions) assuming precisely the same attitudes as their elders, thus guaranteeing that the stalemate continues.

Bono: "You just think of a young guy sitting in watching TV with his family and there's a knock on the door and then the door comes down and British soldiers walk in, turn over the house, maybe his father takes a blow from a rifle butt and that young guy grows up in hatred. Then you cut to another street where there's another boy and another family watching the same TV programme and there's a knock on the door and his Dad who's an RUC man answers it and is blown away on the doorstep. And that young boy grows in hate. Two people polarised with so much in common – that's the tragedy".

Returning to the genesis of "Sunday Bloody Sunday" Bono comments: "Our music is primarily uplifting but at the same time there's a realism to our music as opposed to an escapism, I think, which must acknowledge influences. And it was when I realised that the troubles had not affected me, that it started to affect me. People said "how can you in Dublin write a song about what is happening over the border?" and I didn't know what to say – but the bombs may not go off in Dublin but they're made here.

"And what I was trying to say in that song is: There it is. In close-up. I'm sick of it. How long must it go on?' It's a statement. It's not even saying here's an answer.

"It's just saying — how long must this go on?"

As the night rolls on, our conversation moves into a more general discussion about the value of music, its oft-questioned power to communicate something of importance, its potential to move people, perhaps even to change them.

Bono recalls Dylan: "He said there are two types of music — healing music and music that is destructive. I believe music has great healing.

"Half of me says "I know I can't change the world" and there's another half of me that, every time I write a song I want it to change the world. I don't know if that's naivety or stupidity in me but I do know that music has changed me and I know that in Vietnam music helped change a generation's attitudes. I don't try to change the world, I don't even try to change people – but in the same way I've changed I think other people change too. What's important is the individual, that's where you start. In *Rolling Stone* I said that revolution begins in your heart, in your refusal to compromise your own

> **"Whereas the previous two elpees had been inward-looking, "War" was outward-looking. Whereas the previous two elpees had, in the lyric sense, been impressionistic, "War" was more like graffiti".**

beliefs, and I think that expresses it".

And U-2's contribution? Bono states that he's "interested in revolution" and believes that in terms of what U-2 "stand for in the business, what we have done is truly rebellious".

He mentions artists like Springsteen, Simple Minds and Big Country as "kindred spirits – different music but kindred spirits. We're all dreamers, I suppose.

"People say that a U-2 concert and a Clash concert are similar in terms of reaction" he says, "but I think they're worlds apart. I like the Clash and I like Joe Strummer, I think he's an honest man and I don't want to be hard on them. But sometimes people go to a concert, any concert, and they're nervous. There's tension there and, at some concerts I've been to, the tension is still there at the end when people walk out. A U-2 concert seems to be different, and that's the healing thing, the washing thing. I really believe that rock 'n' roll is very powerful".

Playing devil's advocate, I counter that people might argue that such an experience is a transient one, lasting only for the duration of the concert itself.

"But there's unity for an hour and a half", he replies "musicians can do what politicians can't do and I think those feelings, those communal feelings are quite addictive. You feel that warmth and you go after it. Rock 'n' roll should be a release. If the Garda Siochana realised that at our concerts in Gaiety Green car park, there was a real explosion, a real release, the steam pouring from the valve ... Rock 'n' roll is for that and it's best expressed in music, which is a positive thing, than to express it all over somebody's face in a blow.

"Y'know I want to inspire people and fire up people. You know that thing: "Lie down in your own mess". Our

The Edge

Pic: Anton Corbijn.

U2

Pic: Anton Corbijn.

music is not something to lie down to, to get out of to, to die to, to commit suicide to. It's not a soundtrack to a nervous breakdown. It's music to fire people up so that maybe they will fight back, not again, with sticks and stones but in some other way, some other channel.

"And I think that's a fact, that's real. I know that a lot of good things have happened. Sometimes with U-2 you can end up talking about U-2 in the abstract but the music is very real".

I think you can see that something has come to an end in this group and that certain things have brought that to a head and I really feel that we are about to start again", Bono tells me at one point in our discussion, and, indeed, if there's a central theme around which the night's conversation revolves, it's that of re-appraisal and re-birth.

Again the band's experiences in America, particularly on their most recent three-month tour, have had a notable impact. Bono cites a specific example.

"People are quite aware that there's no stage big enough for me — I like to stretch the stage and I've often found myself singing from the back of the hall rather than the front. I'm always trying to get across, to communicate.

"At the US festival, I climbed to the top of the stage to get to the people at the back — there were 300,000 there — and I put a white flag at the top and it counted as a symbol, a broadstroke to that mass of people.

"But another time I went into the audience in L.A. at a big sports complex — there were about 12,000 people there — with a big white flag, and the flag was torn to shreds and I was nearly torn to shreds.

"I got onto the balcony and I found myself looking down and then I found myself jumping about 20 feet into this sea of people, and they caught me and passed me along from the back until eventually I got up onto the stage nearly naked, wondering "what have I done, what's happened?" Because although the people caught me, some other people jumped off the balcony after and there *was*, but there may not have been, people to catch them. And it was at that stage I had to think — responsibility. I mean, the place had gone berserk — what if somebody had died?

"Also as you know, punks in L.A. are into slamdancing which is quite aggressive and as they were tearing the flag to shreds I found myself getting this guy and slamming him against the wall — I was really going for him. I thought: "what's happening to me?" Again that's all part of the rethink and seeing these three albums as the end of an era".

As is often the case, being abroad has paradoxically also made Bono and U-2 much more aware of their native environment. In a practical sense he speaks of Dublin and Ireland as "an anchor": "I love to live here, I love to play here. I love to record here. So many other groups have left this country — they got out as soon as they got the fare for the boat — but we've stayed".

And as we walk along the beach outside his house at three in the morning he elaborates on his feelings about what it is to be Irish and how it's likely to affect U-2's music.

"My ambition for U-2 has always been to push it to its limits — the most aggressive music ever made and, at the same time the most sensitive, different levels. I woke up a few months ago and found out I was Irish (laughs) and that has made an impact and it's going to make an impact on the music. Because this *is* an Irish group and I'm realising that the very weapons you need are all around you.

"I went to see the film "Bladerunner" which had this city of the 90's very powerfully represented on the screen, a very claustrophobic place, the city reaching right up into the stratosphere. Visually I was impressed but there was something wrong — and it was the music. The music was by Vangelis — and I am a fan of Vangelis — but I was thinking that in the 90's people won't be listening to electronic music — who wants electronic music in an electronic age? I've nothing against synths, contrary to popular belief — it's the machines who play the machines that worry me (laughs).

"But I feel that right now, something is about to happen, in music, in painting, in architecture, everything. Modernism is about to be thrown out the window because in an age that Bladerunner represented, there's a humanity that's needed and the music of the 90's I believe will be ethnic music, black music, soul music, reggae music, cajun music — this will be the music of the future because it has a humanity that city dwellers will need.

"You mentioned about Bruce Springsteen coming to see us — well we went out for dinner and we had this 90 minute row-cum-rap. I was talking about "Nebraska" and saying I believed the reason it was successful was the fragile quality of the music. There were tones and textures in the acoustic guitar and mouth organ, an intimacy, that people hadn't heard for a while. All they'd heard was that snare drum — bash! bash!

"So we used the uileann pipes on "Tomorrow" and there's an incredible power to those reedy instruments — the violin, for example, is the nearest instrument to the human voice. There's a timelessness there. In an era when the hands of the clock are sweeping by so fast, there's a timelessness to those sounds, I'm interested in".

Bono was particularly impressed by Clannad's "Harry's Game" which was played at the end of every date on U-2's last U.S. tour, — "They're doing something that is truly innovative and it inspired us" he says— but, for all his enthusiasm, he's quick to point out that the traditional influence is just one among many which he's currently preoccupied with. Add to it U-2's abiding interest in dance music, and the Edge's aforementioned exploration of Nigerian guitar and your guess about the nature of U-2's next elpee (which incidentally, rumour has it may be produced by Conny Plank) is as good as mine. Or for that matter Bono's.

"I can't tell you where we're about to go but I know that I can't sleep at night with the thoughts of it. I'm so excited about this idea that we've just begun — the way I feel is that we're undertaking a real departure. I can't stop talking about it. It would take about 10 men to hold me down at the moment."

And the final word before breakfast and bed.

"People say we take ourselves too seriously and I might have to plead guilty to that. But really I don't take *myself* seriously, we don't take *ourselves* seriously — but we do take the *music* seriously".■

Liam Mackey
Vol 7 No 15 August 5th, 1983.

Three of the best. Pic: Colm Henry

Larry. Pic: Hennessy.

U2 Triumph

The Phoenix Park Festival,
1983

A FINE day, a generally good-humoured crowd in excess of 20,000 and a bill that gave real meaning to the term "strength in depth": most circumstances at the Phoenix Park last Sunday were as near to perfect as made no difference with only the placement of the stage, and the resultant cramped conditions out front working against optimum enjoyment.

Perfect also were the Crime of the same name, for their appointed role. Faced with the unenviable challenge of opening the proceedings, the Perfect

fire up the audience en masse, their blend of guitar power and Celtic *esprit de corps* was, in places, devastating. "Fields of Fire" and "In A Big Country" in particular raised the temperature another few degrees and the heaving, bopping masses at the front throughout testified to the visceral impact of their music. The unison demand for encores — duly reciprocated — was further confirmation of the fact that Stuart Adamson's troops are already well into what should prove to be a long and illustrious campaign.

Viewing the Eurythmics from 100 yards was deceptive. From that distance, Annie Lennox looked like Fozzie Bear (hair by Chantal of David Marshall's) trying to be Grace Jones. Then she seemed to throw a real temperamental wobbler — one plastic bottle and she angrily launched into a peace and love sermon that wouldn't have disgraced Melanie.

But when they settled down, thankfully the Eurythmics weren't one of those drab disappointments, bands who can't emulate their records on stage. Expert soul re-stylists, Dave Stewart in particular is a most informed guitarist, while Annie Lennox is just as evocative a singer live.

Highlight for me was their version of Lou Reed's "Satellite Of Love" turning it into a real futurist scarf-waver for the Bayern Munich of 2001. But the real question must be when will the Eurythmics return? On this provocative showing, they certainly deserve a closer second view.

Simple Minds came on in the wake of the sudden wave of euphoria which followed the announcement of Eamon Coughlan's victory in Helsinki, but from the outset, it was clear that as far as the Phoenix Park crowd were concerned, the Minds were world beaters in their own right.

The nauseating spectacle of a phalanx of blockheads intimidating a section of the audience away to the left of the stage proved an initial, but thankfully temporary distraction, before one's attention could be firmly focused on the music.

Fronted by the rubbery Jim Kerr — Spiderman poses a speciality — Simple Minds proved that, live, their music is a more consistently meaty proposition than is often the case on record. With the springing, mobile rhythm section of Derek Forbes (bass) and Mel Gaynor (drums) a crucial impetus throughout, the band made the maximum impact on songs like "Promised You a Miracle" and "Glittering Prize" but it was "The American" which provided the set's first bona-fide highlight with Kerr masterminding the vocal passages on the chorus splendidly.

"Premonition" displayed their ability to mix power and sensitivity to hypnotic effect before "Someone

Crime surmounted the difficulties, burgled the hearts and minds of many present and went away with a burgeoning reputation worth its weight in gold. On this showing they are destined to pull off the big one. Just give them time.

Then, more low-key perfection; what better proposition on a hot, sunny afternoon than the sweet, seductive rhythms of good reggae. Steel Pulse provided just that and left everybody feeling groovy!

Big Country, on the other hand, must have left a lot of people feeling drained. The first band of the day to really

U2

Pic: Anton Corbijn.

Somewhere In Summertime" shone down on the crowd with the late evening sun, bringing their set to a close and drawing a tumultuous response. For the encore they launched into "New Gold Dream 81-82-83-84" the best song on the album of the same name and as the beat went crashing they worked in elements of both "Take Me To The River" and Sly Stone's "Higher" routine to bring their performance to an appropriately heady climax. They'll be back ...

Afterwards, Bono's sincerely humbled view of their rapturous reception was that U-2 only had to turn up to triumph — but the band deserved their abundant success as they showed just why they are such a special live force.

Personally I won't forget the departing crowd still singing the refrain from "40" long after the closing theme of "Harry's Game" had faded away. They *will* sing that particular song for a long, long time.

Other immediate memories are of Bono's quicksilver instincts — whether showing his unerring sense and sensitivity in dealing with stage-invaders, dragging his father on for a swift jig, or generously dedicating a song to Jim Reilly whose brother was shot the previous weekend in Belfast.

What makes U-2 is their special balance between ego and egolessness, their ability to blend a fierce attack with a message of self-sacrifice in a song like "Surrender".

Theories another time. For absent friends and faithful departed, their set leaned to a mixture of the ancient and modern, with only three songs from the under-estimated "October".

There were some other moments of magical fulfilment: Bono told us it was the Edge's birthday and the crowd sang "Happy Birthday" to him; it was good to see the guitarist given the reception and recognition he's always deserved.

If this festival was, as Bono insists, the final instalment of U-2 mk 1, the last grateful homecoming from the roads of America, the closing of a circle that began in dens like McGonagle's, U-2 also gave a hint of their future direction with a new song "Party Girl" for the first encore.

Forget the accounts of backstage ligging, they're irrelevant to what happened out front. U-2 is about immersion, an attempt to recover a sense of true ecstasy amid the corrupted rituals of "rock".

However hard the heart beats, it must be open. Ultimately that is the essence of U-2, the offering communicated and so gratefully received at the Phoenix Park. U-2 audiences always leave in hope.■

Bono: a champagne gig. Pic: Colm Henry

Chris Donovan, Bill Graham and Liam Mackey.
Vol 7 No. 16 August 18th, 1983.

It's a Celebration!

Bill Graham reviews "Under A Blood Red Sky"

U-2 HAVE always been candid about refurbishing standard rock values.

Populist but not pop, U-2 have never accepted the creeping elitism of many of their contemporaries that downgraded live performance as a chore, the unavoidable sales-pitch before the return to the studio refuge. Shouting "Showtime" with relish on their route to adulation, for U-2 the release of a live album is no afterthought. "Under a Blood Red Sky" is an inevitable obligation and an essential document.

Recorded this year at American and German dates, "Under A Blood Red Sky" profiles U-2 at the precise point in time when the festival stage has just become their natural environment, when they're no longer the second-best band still seeking favours from the headliners' sound-crew. It finds them in command, invulnerable with one exception.

An album of confident excitement, the work of a band completely secure about their powers, "Under A Blood Red Sky" registers U-2's pride on arrival but its task is not to map out the route behind. This is necessarily a record of culmination but it shouldn't be mistaken as the complete chronicle.

This live album's timing means that it doesn't record the early reckless confusion (intentionally so!) that characterised `U-2's and particularly Bono's initial international campaigns-in-jubilation, when they were careering around the clubs. It taps a more masterful emotion — yet I get my satisfaction searching for the special moments.

Like the new seeds of "Party Girl" and "40". "*How long must we sing this song?,*" U2 inquire on the latter and "Party Girl" is their answer to themselves, never quite shaking off its Police and Darnell antecedents but tantalisingly informal nonetheless, like a grubby leather jacket at an overdressed reception.

This album's also the Edge Orchestra's main feature so far. His execution has been so effortless and his function so accepted that his massive responsibilities are often overlooked. But on "Under A Blood Red Sky", the Edge's ability to ride all the horses — rhythm, lead and melody— in the U-2 circus, becomes evident and often breathtakingly so.

U-2 have been able to avoid the tiresome profanities of guitar rock exactly because the Edge's style isn't vulgarised from a blues base. "The Electric Co." is the furthest he ventures into that type of shattering riffing but the Edge's real moments of glory are on "New Year's Day" and "11 O'Clock Tick Tock", the latter a genuine live development of the Hannett-produced original, pulsating through its final section with the guitarist's jagged, spine-tingling variations.

My only material complaint is the exclusion of "An Cat Dubh". Otherwise, the only track that loses life is "Sunday Bloody Sunday". Without the studio shroudings, it becomes unbalanced, too martial, not enough art — the perennial fate of so many anti-war songs set to a military beat.

"Under A Blood Red Sky", the camera pans on a victor's lap of honour. This album closes accounts, clears unfinished business. For their next, will U-2 change the colour of their skies? ∎

Bill Graham
Vol 7 No. 23 November 25th. 1983

Light a Big Fire

Liam Mackey reviews
"The Unforgettable Fire"

The Unforgettable Fire cover session. Pic: Anton Corbijn.

U-2'S DECISION to choose Brian Eno as producer for their new album was a bold move.

Clearly conceived as a challenge for the band — and indeed for Eno who by his own admission was largely unfamiliar with the band's work prior to this — it gave credence to Bono's post-Phoenix Park declaration that that memorable concert had brought to a close the first full cycle of U-2.

Further emphasising, after three acclaimed studio albums and a live wrap-up souvenir, that U-2 had arrived at a radical point of departure, was Eno's playful but pointed assertion in his interview with Bill Graham one month ago, that the album would introduce "five or six new U-2's" to the world.

All of which means that "The Unforgettable Fire" has a lot to live up to — and it's this listener's verdict that it does so, unequivocally.

Inspired by the life of Martin Luther King, the single "Pride (In the Name of Love)" is a characteristically soaring and uplifting tribute to those who fight for peace and justice. Eminently deserving of its chart

110

success, where it shames the transparent piffle that clutters up much of the hit parade these days, it is, in the context of the album, the sole surviving variation on the band's most familiar *modus operandi.* For the remainder of this journey, existing map co-ordinates are of little immediate relevance.

The opening track "A Sort Of Homecoming" rings the changes loud and clear. The primary colours of yore are here absorbed into a much broader canvas, the totality almost symphonic in its orchestration of sounds (as distinctly opposed to instruments) but without the unnecessary grandiosity that description might imply. There's a subtle but effective Irish undercurrent in both the melody and lyrics while the *"O-coma-way, o-coma-way"* refrain effectively evokes the chorus of "I Will Follow". And it's true, U-2 *have* come a long way.

One of the most significant aspects of "The Unforgettable Fire" is the maturing of Bono's abilities as a lyric writer and singer. Throughout the album his choice of language and use of imagery is rich and imaginative, at times brilliantly so, as in "Promenade", a beautifully embellished love song, that's both spiritual and sensual, and wherein Bono echoes Van Morrison in the line *"up the spiral staircase to the higher ground"*.

And then there's the title-track, possibly the album's shining achievement. The visceral string arrangement scored by Noel Kelehan is superb, as is Bono's vocal including a perfectly integrated falsetto, replete with melodic passages of genuine beauty. "The Unforgettable Fire" brings the band into a different dimension in terms of dynamics, texture and atmosphere.

If U-2 tended on occasion towards stridency in the past, that fault has been eradicated here. "Wire", a frenetic black and blue executioner's song is abrasive but not bruising, while "Bad" and "Indian Summer Sky" eschew the temptation of the anthemic in favour of controlled developments of the music's intrinsic power.

I'm still wrestling with the strange "Elvis Presley And America", in which at one point Bono's treated voice sounds uncannily like Lou Reed and thus far, only "4th Of July", an instrumental that's akin to a slow-motion fireworks display, leaves me cold.

"The Unforgettable Fire" ends with "MLK", again addressed to Martin Luther King. Part elegy, part lullaby, it closes U-2's warmest album yet on an appropriately direct and moving note.

This then, is the beginning of the new chapter of U-2. With an album as rich and rewarding as "The Unforgettable Fire" as an introduction, the possibilities for the future seem limitless.■

Liam Mackey
Vol 8 No. 20 19th October, 1984

Pic: Anton Corbijn.

Quest for Fire

Bill Graham follows U2 and "The Unforgettable Fire" from Slane, Co. Meath to the concert halls of Europe.

rian's the scissors man. He's the man to make the cut". Slane Castle, last May. Over dinner, Bono is whispering confidentially into my tape-recorder after a day's recording there.

The setting is unique, without any of the cramped antiseptic conditions that generally accompany recording. Outside, it's a gloomy, drizzly day but inside as the Edge experiments on some screaming overdubs, U-2 and family are clustered around a roaring heartening fire.

Bono divides his attention between the Edge's activities and his pocket chessboard. The guitarist's wife, Aisling, swollen with the daughter, Holly she'll soon bear, reclines on the couch. Bearing a white U-2 banner, a group of fans from the village gape through windows till they're shooed away. The Edge plays a particularly scalding break and receives the producer's opinion. "That's the least Protestant solo you've ever played" says Brian Eno.

Slane has been turned upside town for U-2's stay. Equipment boxes are scattered everywhere and taped powerlines stretch through the hall to the generator. Essentially the band are using two rooms, the drawing-room where the mobile recording console is located and the library, with its perfect acoustics designed for chamber-music recitals, for the instrumental recording itself.

The old moulds are being most deliberately broken. Nobody really knows where this album's bound but U-2 are convinced they must head toward a new and foreign destination. They have no intention of making "Son Of War".

This departure is no sudden, panicky shift of direction. Nine months earlier just after U-2 have triumphantly left the Phoenix Park stage, Bono buttonholes me and gives the news that it is the end of an era. Resurrection and reincarnation are now the band's aim. U-2 are dead: long live U-2!

The move to Slane is no surprise. The band have become dissatisfied with how recording studios can deaden and depersonalise a band's sound and through the Spring, they have been searching for an alternative venue. Tour manager Dennis Sheehan checks numerous locations and finds Slane has the ideal amenities: perfect acoustics, bed, board, and a restaurant below, a location far enough to remove but not isolate them from Dublin, a setting in historic Meath beside the Boyne to stimulate the imagination and an amenable proprietor in Lord Henry Mountcharles.

Meanwhile the band are discovering that the outlines of the new album are already contrasting with "War". "The material was European rather than American", The Edge will later comment, the band concluding that its character will not suit the crisp production style of Jimmy Iovine who has just overseen "Under A Blood Red Sky". They toy with the notion of giving an invitation to Conny Plank but then seek out and win over Brian Eno who brings with him his Canadian engineer and collaborator, Daniel Lanois. Now all the parts are in place.

Yet this pre-production work wasn't accomplished without some stress. Even Island boss, Chris Blackwell, a man who normally appreciates when his acts must follow their hunch, was worried by the choice of Eno.

Bono recalls an early Dublin meeting with Blackwell: "We said to him "If you're over here because you're concerned about a group that you are a fan of, well then we appreciate that concern and we'll talk to you. But if you're over here guarding your investment, then maybe you should leave now". And he said "No" ... and he ended up leaving as a fan and with a better idea of what we were trying to do".

For myriad reasons, U-2 must make this break. Even should the album be a comparative commercial failure, indeed even should it be some artistic mish-mash, it is a necessary exercise.

For even though it will be their fifth album and their first under a new Island contract, U-2 are still a young group and one at a hazardous crossroads. If they churn out xeroxes of "War", they may satisfy the powerbrokers of the American music business but they will be vampirized, a band with its creative blood sucked dry, increasingly dispirited and likely headed for a

Pic: Colm Henry

rancorous split in the medium-term. Alternatively they can renew themselves, using all the ideas and experiences accumulated through their career, to chart a new course that will sustain U-2 for the remainder of the decade.

There is another paradoxical reason why they must switch now. A change delayed may be too late. It is exactly at the first peak of their appeal that a band can most easily strike out and acclimatise their audience to their new desires. In a year or more, U-2 might be typecast and trapped by a trademark sound, paralysed by their audience's demand for more of the same. It is the select few who strike out and win; U-2 wish to join that breed.

Slane Castle, sipping his peppermint tea, gazing at the arcane symbols on his strategy blackboard that record the progress of each track while Danny Lanois smilingly coaxes The Edge to further pyrotechnics in the library.

Relaying the reasoning behind U-2's new policy, Bono reminds of the band's beginnings: "It's probably regression rather than progression in some ways because it's what we started out doing. We started out as a group innovating in the three-piece format. I don't want to sound pompous but that's how we started, we wrestled with that. Whereas "War" was a deliberate stripping-down into the three-piece format".

At last, my tape is stored away. Bono changes his guise, leading the company assembled at the dinner-table through a massed chorus of "Come Back Ronald Reagan To Ballyporeeen". All bands have their rituals to release the pressure. At Slane, this comic anthem is U2's

Of course, it took longer than planned. The original scheme was to cut the fundamental tracks at Slane and then just add decorative overdubs at Windmill before mixing there. But U-2 were still sculpting in September.

The Edge can now reflect on the reasons: "When you switch to a new location, it tends to take a couple of weeks to get in to the momentum of the new creative surrounding. We recorded a lot of stuff in Slane which we had to re-evaluate and in some cases re-record. We had to find out whether we had what we thought we had and in some cases we didn't and that was sad. In some cases, we had done great work — far better than we had thought — and that was rewarding. So I suppose it was just the fact that we did record in two halves".

Obsessively perfectionist, U-2 might still be ensconced in Windmill if Eno hadn't had to depart for his own projects or if the group hadn't been contracted to their first Australian tour in October.

But the delay primed them for a hectic schedule. In barely a fortnight, the band posed for Anton Corbijn's cover photos, shot the video for "Pride", rehearsed their new set and spoke to the teams of European and Australian press who were being couriered through Windmill. Other minor business matters competed for their attention. As the promotional machine was wound up for "Unforgettable Fire", the sense of strain was not always faint.

But it was more than tempered by a sense of achievement. A moody almost mystical album that contrasts with the muscular exhortations of "War", "Unforgettable Fire" met their own expectations.

The alliance with Eno and Lanois had worked. Only one track, "Indian Summer Sky" with its hints of Eno's former clients, David Bowie and Talking Heads, finds U-2 overly-subjected to outside forces.

Brian had correctly identified U-2's "abundance of lyrical soul". Before on "October", both their most misjudged and unfinished album, those moods are fitfully sketched. On the title track, they distilled that spirit but on "Tomorrow", they let a philistine guitar depth-charge the yearning conveyed by Vinnie Kilduff's pipes and Bono's vocal. Such inexperienced errors are avoided on "Fire".

The record takes U-2 into their own modern mystic, besides confirming Eno's view that there are "4 or 5 U-2's on it." "MLK" is their lullaby, "Bad" calls on both Van

Pic: Anton Corbijn.

Pic: Colm Henry

memories of the deaths of his family in Auschwitz. A member of no sect, perhaps that impossible but profound contradiction of our culture, an agnostic desperate for mystic belief, Celan may have been the foremost European spiritual poet of the century. Among his lines was this maxim: *"Poetry is a sort of homecoming"*.

Which isn't to claim that Celan permeates all the album but it does show the error of rigidly defining U2. True believers may hold firmly to the distinctions but there is a slim line between the saint, the seer and the holy sinner. "Fire"'s true worth is that U-2 are finally adultly communicating across those barriers, unreeling a thread to the unconverted and pressing beyond the arid formalities of institutionalised practice. On "Homecoming", they start to find the tongue of charged archetypes. *"Once more in the name of love"*, U-2 herald the law that must bind all, believers or not.

They should not be trivially tagged. Nor Bono either. To the unsympathetic, he can seem a yappy man but that misleading view forgets his attentiveness, his ability to trap and store ideas 'till they have fertilised in his mind. You do not perform so regularly to so many with such accurate intensity, unless you possess and develop acutely-tuned instincts.

Thus the other side of U-2. In the studio, they had switched. Could that change be transferred to stage? One journeyed to Europe to discover the answer.

If they order things differently in France, it is not to the benefit of live rock 'n' roll. Successive French governments may be proud of their cultural policies but you can't boogie in the Pompidou Centre. Lacking suitable venues, U-2 have joined the circus, playing a succession of tents through France.

Even Paris is deprived so on a murky, rainy evening, I'm driven to the Escape Baclard where a huge tent has squatter's rights in a dilapidated space that will ultimately be invaded by the re-developers. Outside, chestnut sellers ply their trade. A few exotic hippies, specimens who seem to have only been preserved on the Continent (*and in West Cork — Ed*) are sighted. For a second, I think I'm back in '74, fully expecting Donovan, Arthur Brown and Manfred Mann's Earth Band to pop up as support.

These longhair diehards are the only splash of rock fashion. The French aren't tribal about their music as they believe rock regalia spoils their own chic gear. Merchandisers do little business here so there's an absence of badges or tee-shirts to check the loyalties of the U-2 audience.

There must be 8,000 on the premises but conditions are far from ideal. Inside I immediately feel droplets of

Morrison and the Velvet Underground — an apparently odd couple 'till U-2 made the match — while "Elvis Presley In America" ("it's like watching a dress-rehearsal from off-stage," says The Edge) catches Bono improvising to a slowed-down track.

(An aural hint. That cut bears inspection at 45rpm. It may chipmunk the singer but the test does give an approximation of the original instrumental track).

But it is both the title track and "A Sort of Homecoming" that should deflect any charge that their Christian ties have stifled the sweep of U-2's romantic imagination.

Or censored the sources from which they derive inspiration. Three years back on their first American "Boy" tour, a friend lent Bono a "Penguin Modern Poets" copy of the poetry of Paul Celan, a Roumanian-born but German-speaking Jew who in 1970 committed suicide in Paris, tortured by the mutilating condensation from the tent's roof on my shoulder. Though I don't yet know it, this has been a frustrating day for band and crew. At the sound check, rain had been seeping through gaps in the canopy. This is one gig to be played on a wing and a prayer.

Past nine and the taped strains of "4th Of July" announce U-2's arrival. I see a set most unlike the one they displayed at the Phoenix Park. Much is intended but some is improvised. In this Parisian super-marquee, U-2 have to bluff like they're playing a summer festival in Ballina.

They start with "11 O'Clock Tick Tock" and "I Will Follow", then move to a brace from the new album, "Wire" and the soothing ceremonial of "MLK". But on "Unforgettable Fire" they meet the first trip-wire as the Edge's keyboards pack up. "'Unforgettable Fire' with the forgetful keyboards", Bono jests afterwards.

They just manage to cover their retreat but Bono is now clearly discontented, complaining about the closed tent-flaps that increase the heat and condensation. Michael Deeny, former Horslips manager with a business foothold in France who's co-promoting these French dates, demurs. "I've already ordered them all open", he claims not without some taint of exasperation.

Bono's too sharp not to involve the audience. "I don't mind if it rains on me but the sun is coming out for us" he shouts. The French cheer and "Two Hearts Beat As One" is closed with a quote from Ann Peebles' "I Can't Stand The Rain".

So far — with the pardonable exception of "Unforgettable Fire" — it's been a strong show, U-2 cruising at the high performance altitudes to which they're accustomed but now on "Electric Co." Bono chucks in his stick of gelignite and hi-jacks the show.

This *coup de theatre* is wholly unexpected. Suddenly Bono bursts out "Jesus (pronounced in the Spanish style) where did it go when you don't know?" searing down to a new layer of meaning in the song.

Later backstage I will get the complete story of a friend incarcerated in a mental hospital who thought himself Jesus and was subjected to Electro-Convulsive Therapy (ECT). "The doctors can sometimes produce an effect but they don't know the cause. ECT, it's nothing more than witchcraft", he'll complain.

Thus "1-2-3, Electric Co." And as he acts out the ECT experience, complete with head-jerking machine, I'm rivetted and startled by this gamble, this raw uncovering of emotional nakedness, far from rock's usual over-rehearsed gambits, that propels the show to a higher plane. It is the one jagged outcrop of the night.

Michael Deeny returns and good-naturedly recants: "He was right. All the flaps weren't opened. When you give the French an order, they form a committee and think about it. I had to do it myself".

Pic: Colm Henry

By now, the condensation has forced the crew to put plastic coverings over both the sound and light desks. God knows what it's like on stage but the only signs of distress are the keyboards clanking in the upper registers of "October" and the number of guitars the Edge keeps swopping. Through it all, Adam Clayton keeps beaming benevolently.

This *is* a different show. Bono abstains from mountaineering over the amps and sprinting round the stage.

"Banging the door down, that's the image I used to Dave McCullough five years ago but it was like we'd smashed the door down and it was open and we were

> **"I remember saying 'Yes, I've got to stop it.' And then, the next time, walking on stage and walking on the balcony again, really hoping to fall, hoping that I'd end the tour."** —
> *Bono*

still banging away", Bono had reflected on their live shows, pre-"Unforgettable Fire".

"And I was the culprit. There was this complete overdose in America in front of 12,000 people at the Los Angeles Sports Arena when I jumped off a balcony. It was disgraceful. I went into the audience with the white flag and it was a manic audience that ripped me and the flag apart.

"I ended up attacking this guy, flooring this guy in the audience. I was about 20 feet from the stage, right up in the balcony and I was in a fracas with a member of my own audience. I mean it's a white flag and I'm going ... phootf ... completely with the adrenalin. Then I went down and I said "Look, I'm going over the balcony" and I did. It was 20 feet below.

"And there was this writer and he said — I can't remember the actual phrase — he'd never seen such an act and he didn't know if he wanted to see it again. As much as he was in awe of the performance, he thought it was frightening in its implications. Back in the dressing room, the band said "we've got to stop this". I remember saying "Yes, I've got to stop it". And then the next time, walking on stage and walking on the balcony again, really hoping to fall, hoping that I'd end the tour.

"I think it was all down to lack of confidence in the music as the expression as opposed to the act as the expression".

Later The Edge would elaborate: "That wasn't a turning-point, so much as one of the instances that led us to the conclusion that this was an avenue we should abandon as soon as possible. I didn't think it was us. I didn't think it really reflected what we were about. I felt it undermined the dignity and nobility of the music. There's a sort of special feeling and mood to it, a subtle thing and what was going down in some of the shows was melodramatic and bombastic.

"I think it was the result of the intense emotional trauma of being on stage and seeing an audience of that size and trying to present what you do. It's very hard and not something I will ever understand. For Bono, it's an incredibly difficult thing to do. He doesn't have an instrument, he's out there ..."

His instrument is his instinct?

"It's 'something to hide behind as well, sometimes (*smiles*) ... it's technique, it's something to do. He couldn't help himself in a lot of cases and I think he works best when he's in control. When he loses it, I don't think it's in the spirit of what we're doing anymore".

Now U-2 use their music to make the hall smaller. For all the praise lavished on their live show, the word "party" has been rarely used, yet tonight it's in the frame of reference. Without depreciating the force of the music, U-2 are putting on a much friendlier performance than any I've seen.

There's new security. Now they aren't afraid to show their humour as at the encore "Party Girl" when Bono introduces the Edge as Jimi Hendrix and his guitar packs up again. "He wants a new guitar for Christmas" Bono quips mischievously to a Parisian crowd long since converted. The U-2 busking team doesn't miss a trick.

Later Bono will reflect on a night when rain and condensation were always threatening. "If ... had to cope with this, they would have collapsed" he says, identifying a band born not a million miles from Liverpool. Instead this date has blooded the tour as they've bluffed, busked, pulled rabbits out of the hat and used all the experience that comes courtesy of an early apprenticeship amid Kiltimagh productions.

Backstage the court gathers, evidence that a band which can rouse these Parisians is now going global. The band are highly satisfied by their Houdini act and Bono's sufficiently relaxed to affectionately recall an earlier night in the tour when after a lacklustre show, Adam had read him the riot act, reminding him that, "you, Bono are responsible for the morale of this band".

The band submit to protocol, gain the praises of Jean Paul Goude, former partner of Grace Jones whom Chris Blackwell thinks might embellish their stage design and then politely disengage themselves for a meal at a club. The days of self-protection are past. Though U-2 may not follow the Motorhead Guide To Road Etiquette, the days when socialising was limited to Adam Clayton and manager Paul McGuinness are behind them. Now Bono admits he needs these hours to let his batteries run

118

down.

So at the restaurant table, Bono and the Edge sit, joke, discuss Bruce Springsteen and allied topics and listen while Michael Deeny regales us with stories from his back pages. The night before, the pair had ventured into the night-club connected to the restaurant and witnessed the Monaco princesses, France's only royalty, surrounded by their nightlife court. All they can talk of is the transparancy of it all.

They depart. I wander into the club and find the pair have marked my cards: Paris night-life is not what it's cracked up to be. Though the music's good, the Parisians' notion of dancing is to vaguely flap their arms while tepidly cruising around the floor. Nothing down there for dancing, I hope the princesses have it up there for thinking. Ah well, to bed. The next stop is Brussels.

And the Vost National. Now the tour returns to conventional halls and this ideal Brussels venue, a round amphitheatre that allows maximum communication between group and the 8,500 attendance. As the Alarm finish, the anticipation is palpable. Besides the Belgians, there's a German contingent plus coachloads of English followers who've crossed the Channel for their Saturday night out with U-2.

The yeast in the loaf, the English intensify the atmosphere. With no technical restrictions in the first decent hall of the tour, U-2 are primed for a concert that ends with their traditional celebration of a special night, the uncorking of champagne during "Party Girl". By the closing "40", Bono's ad-libbing through "Knocking On Heaven's Door" completing a set that flowed with effortless fervour. Any melodrama has been foresworn as absolutely unnecessary.

Well not entirely. Bono retains part of the head-snapping E.C.T. mime through "Electric Co." And on "Sunday Bloody Sunday" though he gathers an Irish tricolour around him, he makes is abundantly clear it should never be a symbol of aggression.

U-2 also dispel doubts I've carried from Paris. There due to the technical gremlins, I didn't learn if they could translate the new orchestral tracks live. But here both "A Sort Of Homecoming" and "Unforgettable Fire" work and when the cigarette-lighters make a luminous necklace 'round the hall during "MLK" I know the new material has been approved.

There may be a further reason for tonight's quality. Alison and Aisling, respectively Bono and the Edge's wives, have flown over with Sheila, Adam's girl-friend, so it's a contented family gathering that later sits down to the small dinner party hosted by Ariola, the record company who distribute Island through the Benelux nations.

I'm seated opposite Larry Mullen. The member who evades the publicity machine, Larry's the one who most regularly and informally slopes off to Dublin gigs, anything from AC/DC to an aspiring local pub band. He also monitors the affairs of their fan club and before our meal, he's been gently confiding in a group of Belgian fans gathered in the hotel lobby.

He's proud of the band's new musical accomplishments. As the Edge relates: "I think the experience of working with Brian and Danny was a revelation to him. Instead of his goal being technique and pure drumming ability, I think he's now far more aware of new approaches, new set-ups to drumming. He's got a very unique combination of drums now with a few different snares and timbales right in there with his main kit".

As U-2's man in the street, Larry's well-equipped to counter the flak U-2 now sometimes receive from their juniors in Dublin: "Everybody's got their own tastes so I can't expect everyone to like the band. But I'd hope they'd respect our achievement".

Yet if Larry Mullen has the lowest profile in Europe and America, in Japan and Australia he was the teenybopper's choice. Apparently at one Australian concert, the girls were almost scrambling past Bono to get their hands on the blond drummer.

Tonight, moreover, is the rhythm section's night since they walk off with the two gold discs presented by Ariola. Adam makes a brief speech and takes the Michael, pretending he'll melt down the disc towards the cost of

> **The member who evades the publicity machine, Larry's the one who most regularly and informally slopes off to Dublin gigs, anything from AC/DC to an aspiring local pub band.**

a new car. We leave with another Irish joke. Signing the guest-book, we note an earlier Irish entrant, Chris De Burgh. "Slainte", he's written, "that means Guinness tastes different in Ireland".

Perhaps he suffered some European ailment. Throughout the tour U-2, bar Adam who figures alcohol kills the bugs, have been suffering minor tummy troubles and since Paris, the Edge has been fighting a cold. His voice is firm but both the flu and antibiotics have weakened him.

It's a less lively crew that drive to the second night's show and when Bono introduces the Edge for his vocal showcase on "Seconds" he says he's "someone we had to take here tonight on a stretcher. Will you welcome a very sick man?"

The crowd is satisfied by a solid show. U-2 maintain a high average beneath which they don't fall but, after the Edge has been sped back to his doctor and bed, both Adam and Bono are highly self-critical.

They need no prompting from mise. Adam complains that it was very "kick-ass" and wants no arena Americanisms creeping into the set — whereas Bono thinks that "Paris was internal from the heart, last night was internal and external, both band and fans but tonight was external only, just the fans".

And in the hall's kitchen, he talks about how he's forging a new stage method, how he's constantly seeking new tricks and how sometime soon, he'd like to talk more to the audience.

Yet their fans don't nit-pick. Two hours later, I sip a beer in an empty Brussels disco before suddenly there arrives a sprinkling of U-2 followers, complete with identifying tee-shirts and jackets. The disc-jockey plays 5 successive U-2 tracks and they're dancing in seventh heaven. "Unforgettable Fire" is number one in Belgium. Obviously these Lowlanders believe they've got a fine bargain.

There are no troughs in Rotterdam. My first experience of Holland and the Dutch civic sense is admirable. Bombed because of its docks to rubble in the Second World War, Rotterdam had to be rebuilt. But its citizens made few of the errors that ravage Dublin. Between its trams and cycle-lanes, Rotterdam is a pedestrian's paradise.

There's also character in the faces on the streets. In Paris along the Champs D'Elysee, the women are so chicly made-up and armoured in fashion, that they seem to have mislaid their spirit. But the Dutch women's faces are alive and individual.

An independent nation, these Dutch. In Cromwell's time their ships raided the Thames and comprehensively embarrassed the British Navy in a war the English never mention. Musically they set the standards of Europe. With their peculiar combination of good taste and bloody-mindedness, the Dutch made Randy Newman a pop star and on morning radio, I hear Roxy Music, the Icicle Works, a smattering of tasty soul including Fontella Bass' "Rescue Me" and of course, "Unforgettable Fire". It goes without saying that the Dutch were the first continentals to support U-2.

Bono has his line: "The city conducts its own symphony" and the Dutch, a robust but not macho race, seem to have an enviable set of priorities. After the second Brussels date, U-2 are already highly motivated but as we travel to the Ahoy venue for the sound-check, all omens seem positive.

The sound-check is more Feedback's Greatest Hits than U-2. The Mount Temple School and Marching Band have, after years of perseverance, finally mastered the covers they used to dismember in their teenage guise and they ricochet through versions of Neil Young's "Southern Man" and "Hurricane" and Led Zep's "Rock 'n' roll". Then the instrumentalists fine-tune while Bono wanders across to Cathy, one of their most devoted fans.

An American based in London, Cathy's already been to Paris. She even saved up to follow U-2 'round Australia. The group now ensure she always gets a backstage pass.

Bono stays on; he wants to view the Alarm. Back in the hotel, Adam plays me a few rough sketches for future songs. Paris had its benefits; both were concocted at the sound-check there.

The first seems a rather stiff funk work-out but the second has real potential with Adam initiating an African pattern that also has a touch of the Irish jaunting cars, as Larry settles behind him. "The Edge may have a synth but he never gets a typical synth sound" he cautions me before the keyboards lock in with textures closer to a hybrid of electric piano and bubbling steel drums. Bono contributes a vocal drone and I concur with Adam when he says "that's one for the library".

The approach may seem haphazard but it can unearth gold dust. For instance, they discovered the essence of "Pride" in ten minutes at a Hawaii sound-check. "Perhaps Island should send us there more often" Adam remarks with relish.

As the Edge comments: "Many other groups, certainly the older ones, tend to start with a chord sequence, melody or even a lyric whereas we tend to sculpt in mood. It might be just a four-bar section. Adam might have a chord sequence and Larry suddenly plays a particularly unusual drumline and we go "Yeah, hang on, there's something different here.

"So I start working on the guitar and there's this overall vision of where this piece might end up. It's not that we would sit down and actually say 'right, this is the chord sequence, this is the guitar or vocal melody, now we have to figure out what the drums and bass will play'. It's a much more instinctive way. It could come from any source in the band, it could even be a mistake. I think Eno works a lot like that, from improvisations".

Yet more conventional methods can also be applied. The Edge explains that "Unforgettable Fire" was formed from "a soundtrack piece I'd been messing around with on the piano at home. It wasn't designed for any particular purpose. I thought it worked well as a film soundtrack, it was a beautiful piece of music but I couldn't see how one would approach it lyrically or vocally.

"I was knocking around for quite a while and myself

120

and Bono were out in his house doing work on material for the record and I found this cassette of the piano piece and we decided to mess around with it. I had the DX 7 keyboard and worked on a treatment and suddenly, there was this very tangible identity. Within about an hour, we'd written a verse section with Bono playing bass and we virtually wrote the song there. Obviously it changed with drums and bass and in the studio, we worked on orchestration — but it was that first 20 minutes in Bono's house that counted. But it was the mood we were always in touch with, not necessarily the chords or the melody".

We drive to the hall and Adam is chided by the Edge for throwing away his spare but unusable continental coins. The exchange prompts a reminiscence from the bassist: "I remember at the start when we used to call around to Paul's home and we didn't have the money for the bus fare back. He used to have this drawer for spare change and we used to raid it. I don't think he quite liked it then".

At the hall, Barry Devlin who's directing a tour video, ambles around, lauding the crew, particularly Steve, their daredevil American rigger. His praise is well-merited. The crew deserve their own paragraph. With English and Americans added to the Irish core who've

been with U-2 since the start, they personify one of Graham's immutable laws of rock 'n' roll: "A band is only as good as its crew".

In my memory, these two Rotterdam dates blend into one, though the second is slightly superior to the first. By now, I'm discovering how "Bad" has grown on me, relishing the Edge's guitar bursts on "Electric Co." and "New Year's Day" and gleefully awaiting Bono's latest stage trick.

First night, he pretends to love the microphone on "11 O'Clock", lets it fall and spontaneously kisses roadie Greg when he recovers it. Then on "Gloria" he invites a girl up from the crowd, jokes, "I can't dance like I used to" and then sweeps her over his shoulder, Tarzan-style from the stage.

Second night, there's a scent of the old Bono, a tremor of fear as he goes off the stage, up onto the cyclepath that divides the audience. The element of risk remains but "Two Hearts Beat As One" caps it.

He's given both a Union Jack and a Tricolour and wraps the English flag around him in a signal of detente. There's the faintest hiss, an understandable desire to support the Irish underdog but Bono won't be mistaken. He flings both flags away. "I get tired with all these flags, Union Jack and Green, White and Orange, Stars and Stripes and Hammer and Sickle".

Such moments kill any staleness in the set, prevent it

121

from congealing into formality. Every night, U-2 have to clean the mirror, prevent the spectacle from taking them over. It's only one facet their critics miss. So many people stick themselves in so many reality-tunnels when they view this band.

U-2 are a rather more complex and paradoxical entity than their detractors realise. They see only America, Christianity, success and arena rock, account the band a perfect post-punk package for Reaganland and don't peer further.

They disregard U-2's control. They miss the fact that U-2 are among the elect who have achieved the oft-expressed but rarely accomplished aim of making the business work for them. While the ABC's and Heaven 17's were poring over their press-releases, U-2 were getting up early in the morning.

But bands must not only harness the business, they must also never be suffocated by their audience. With "Unforgettable Fire", U-2 have escaped the demands for bludgeoning guitar heroism and unlocked the door to further development. That too takes control.

U-2 are now dealing with the hardest music spheres beyond rock 'n' roll's earthly, secular, social, physical functions. The seventies got it badly wrong (there are still creatures who believe the Moody Blues introduced "The Cosmic Rock Revolution") and the mass-marketing of hippie mysticism and spurious cult — God wasn't just an astronaut, he was the conductor on the 15A — was a blight on the era whose soundtrack was often vacuous mood music imprisoned by outmoded Victorian aesthetics.

There must be a music of the spirit that doesn't repeat those errors, that seeks the kernel not the shell. This, I suspect is U-2's future task.

But U2's Christianity is at the heart of their paradox. Exactly because it is unapologetic, the band's critics get blinded by the glare and take it for granted. There is some case to be made that "War"'s clanging hard rock attack sometimes led to undue pulpit-thumping. Equally some may discern that their beliefs performed the useful early function of steering them away from the reefs of rockbiz corruption — but that still doesn't take us to the heart of the matter.

Oddly, blacks be they still soul or reggae artists, are permitted Christian values but white rockers only gain tolerance and/or bemused credit if they're Buddhists, scientologists or members of some other fashionably arcane sect. Their critics never endow U2's Christianity with any rock 'n' roll magic.

Yet it means U-2 enter rock from an odd and creatively stimulating angle particularly now they have the maturity and the experience that admits a growing

sense of moral complications. What should never be forgotten is that U-2 are far beyond the shadow-play of formal belief.

Further, somebody has to court the Americans in their arenas. Now that the USA has opted for a further spell of Reagan illusion, bands like U-2 may give some small but not trivial aid in building a bridge back to reality.

The challenge of the arenas can't be refused. Hell, we are talking about "popular music" here and alongside any "War On Pop" must also be an equal assault on encrusted ideas of "anti-pop".

U-2 confuse on two counts. Patently they can't be numbered among the fashion serfs beholden to their feudal lords but neither do they involve themselves with

Pic: Colm Henry

122

any current modish fastidiousness, the amateur indie ethic, the refusal to compete that leads to so many downcast, under-invested acts. Somebody has to meet the challenge with all possible positive force, crank up the machine and see if music can still move crowds of 8,000 with the least compromise. Few better men than U-2 for the job.

One final Rotterdam memory. "Party Girl" finds the imp in Bono spraying the Edge with champagne, both collapsing in mirth and barely holding the song together. But the bubbly's really for Larry, 23 today on Hallowe'en.
The man who pinned the notice to the school board

is symmetrically last to leave the stage, pounding out his piece as the chant of "40" reverberates around the hall. Clannad's "Harry's Game" completes the closing ritual, the acknowledgement that as long as U-2 hold to the purity of Irish melody, they can evade the hollowness of a new pomp-rock.

Let Paul Celan have the last line: "There are still songs to be sung on the other side of humankind". ∎

Bill Graham
Vol 8 No 23, November 30th, 1984.

This is The Edge

The Edge comes out from behind the guitar.
Interview: Bill Graham

"Something Keith Richards said: 'This is what I do and I do it well. There are people who play guitar better but there's nobody who does it as well as me because I am me.' There's nobody as good at being Keith Richards as Keith Richards. There's nobody as good at being U-2 as U-2".

He avoids saying there's nobody as good at being The Edge as The Edge. A man who lets his work speak, The Edge is both well-mannered and self-contained, completely contrasting with Bono's constant urge to self-exposure. But watch him spin a tale and you'll see the sparkle in his eyes.

He must possess a submerged wayward streak to break the rules and role of a rock guitarist in the way the Edge has done. Even as a youngster taking piano lessons, he did it his way.

"I studied it for two years, then packed it in at the ripe old age of 13 and didn't look at it 'till the "Boy" sessions. I always had a good ear. I never used to read the music. I'd just figure it out. But that was no good because the idea was to read the dots and I could never get that together. It was like teaching arithmetic to somebody who already had a calculator".

Though there were no professional musicians in the Evans family, his father was and is a member of the Dublin Welsh Male Voice Choir. Besides, his elder brother Dik, a later Virgin Prune, was also a member of the U-2 baby-band.

"We bought equipment together. I owned half a guitar and half an amp, which was kind of difficult since there were two guitar-players and they owned half a guitar each. So we used to borrow another guitar and use the same amp".

His developing style became the reason his brother left: "As a guitar player, I've always done the work of two. One of the reasons Dik left was because two guitar players never worked. I never had that discipline. I was always filling up every spare moment with guitar".

Now he believes "it was a musical instinct to make that tapestry. It wasn't a conscious decision that it was the way to go. It was purely intuitive, that idea of a line, a continuous train of thought through the song".

The combination with Adam Clayton's basslines was also an influence: "His wasn't a very bottomy sound and his playing wasn't with lots of gaps a la black funk bass players. It was a quite continuous sound in its own right. That led me to adopt a similar style and also to stick to the higher registers of the guitar where there was a certain gap between the two instruments and a clarity as a result".

Since then, he's evolved multiple musical abilities, using keyboards and lap steel. Working with Brian Eno, he learnt there were similarities in their approaches:

"I could see how Eno had shaped his career not around any one particular overriding talent but through a collection of, I suppose you would say second-rate, abilities. But the way he used them, that he'd been so determined to follow the areas in music he found stimulating to create a career — that must be totally unique.

"Now I don't think I'm a particularly talented guitar virtuoso. My talent if it's anything is my approach to the guitar by the use of effects, by non-acceptance of the usual approaches to the guitar".

Like all the group, the Edge is insistent that Daniel Lanois also receives due credit: "He's a very good reputation in Canada. He's been voted producer of the year for a few years in a Canadian music paper. They worked very much as a team. They didn't separate their tasks. I think Danny, because of his particular talent with notation and manuscript music, was able to communicate with us in a very specific way that Steve Lillywhite never could and never tried to. I'm talking about arrangements in particular, drumlines and guitars. He was very good on rhythm. He plays very good funk guitar and I think he and Larry got on very well".

He says Eno and Lanois "were constantly setting precedents about the sessions. Brian would say something like "these speakers don't inspire me. They have a particularly hard sound and this is the second mix we've had difficulty with. Let's make the decision now and bring in some new speakers". Now our attitude would have been, "Ah, I'm sure they're alright. Kinda Irish, not following through on an instinct. They had

The Edge in Slane Castle during "The Unforgettable Fire" sessions. Pic: Colm Henry

great follow-through. I would choose a guitar to play a certain part and Danny would say "Well Edge, that guitar sounds nice but that guitar over there, I've noticed whenever you've played it, it inspires you. Why don't you use that one?"

The Edge rates Robert Fripp, Adrian Belew, Holger Czukay and particularly "Marquee Moon" era Tom Verlaine as his favourite fellow guitarists. He's also a film buff, with a hankering to write soundtracks: "It's more the cinematography rather than the theatre/drama side. Stanley Kubrick's "Barry Lyndon", that sort of thing really interests me".

Boy Dylan once called Robbie Robertson "a mathematical guitar genuis", a description which also seems to fit the Edge's goldcrested style. I hope it won't damage his modesty. Most times I asked the Edge about himself, he kept pulling back to "we", the community of the band. He seems to huddle aside from fame. "I cannot ever really comprehend what our fans see me as", he says, "I can only observe it from the eye of the storm".

"Probably the people who buy our records or go to our shows are far more aware of the Edge as the public person than I am. I happen to be more aware of his private side".

Thus the Edge: the semi-detatched guitar hero.■

Bill Graham
Vol 8 No. 23 November 15th, 1984

Portrait of the guitar-hero by Colm Henry

The Unforgettable Fire

**Niall Stokes sees U2 light up Madison Square Garden
in New York.**

The Edge close to the edge. Pic: Colm Henry

material, with a conviction that would have been rare in much more experienced outfits. That clear-sightedness and defiant sense of purpose has been a hallmark of their work since then.

From their earliest sightings, there was a ring of authenticity, of longevity, of some vast potential to U-2's music. To feel the atmosphere in a packed Madison Square Garden, to watch the flaming lighters held aloft from the 20,000 strong army of U-2 fans in the audience, to hear the mighty rounds of applause, the thunderous wave of a mass emotional release as they walk on stage, one by one, is to realise that that magic is still there — only magnified 100-fold!

As they crash into the opening riff of "11 O'Clock Tick Tock", New York goes ape. The audience in the Big Apple is notoriously among the most difficult in the world to convert, but they've fallen head over heels in love with U-2 and there's no holding back now. In a seated venue, we're on our feet from the word go and the floor of Madison Square Garden is moving a solid foot up and down under the dancing forces. It's a wild celebration that's sustained through ninety exhausting minutes of sheer musical fervour ...

A storming "I Will Follow" is next, completing a brace of early classics — delivered nowadays with the power and authority of a supremely integrated musical task force. Then it's through to the "War" album and a message addressed by Bono, in his introduction, to the President of the United States, Ronald Reagan. "*It takes a second to say goodbye!*" the Edge sings centrestage and the band pound into one of their funkiest vehicles, a pressure cooker topped with a heavyweight, compulsive chant.

Bono describes "2 Hearts Beat As One" as a love song about how it should be, introducing a more tender note into a gig that's so far been notable for its toughness, its muscle. But it's with the healing lullaby "MLK", directed to the spirit of the late black civil rights leader Martin Luther King, that U-2's range begins to reveal itself fully. It's a haunting and beautiful piece of music, quiet and melancholy, the Irish inflections in the melody lending it a distinctive grace: lighters flare all around the vast expanses of The Garden, a moment where ritual and symbolism meet with a unique sense of appropriateness. "*If the thundercloud passes rain, so let it rain, rain on me*", Bono sings and the deep resonance of the music achieves a cleansing purity. "*Sleep, sleep tonight and may your dreams be realised*". It's an emotional calm, a moment of lucid evanescence shot through with a tender vein of optimism.

Then to the ambitious soundscapes of "Unforgettable Fire". There's no string section in attendance but the melody aches as lovingly live as on record and Bono is delivering the plea with feeling: "*Stay, stay with me*

I t's a long way from Limerick Civic Week to Madison Square Garden but U2 have made that transition — and in such magnificent style

It was back in 1978 that the band made their first dent on the consciousness of the world's music-loving public by winning the pop section of Limerick Civic Week's talent competition. It was, needless to say, a small dent — an infinitesimal dent even! But for the four school-going kids who had played only a handful of gigs previously, it was as significant an affirmation as they could possibly have hoped for, at that fledgling stage in their musical development.

Doubtless that first sweet taste of success fuelled their hunger for more. Equally, it must have fuelled their commitment to a vision which is entirely and uniquely their own. They won that contest performing original *tonight*". He doesn't have to ask: in any context it's one of U-2's finest achievements.

It's a reflection of U-2's maturity that such a wide range of emotional pastures are covered with such evident poise. And that the crowd are carried with them every step of the way: the attention never dissipates, the response is never less than highly charged and there's an incredible absence of fans trying desperately to dictate what should be next. For Madison Square Garden tonight, U-2 can do no wrong.

An electric "Wire", is followed by "Sunday Bloody Sunday", the opening strains of which are greeted with rapturous applause. A tricolour bearing the legend U-2

> **"Pride (In The Name Of Love)"... is a highly dramatic, moving end to a set that's been worked and honed, 'till it sparkles and shines, diamond bright and twice as nice.**

on the white section is passed up through the audience to Bono, and then another. He drapes them over the mike, and covers them with a white flag: it's a risky moment in that the gesture could be interpreted negatively. But it's a statement for peace and reconciliation , against bigotry, that accurately reflects the sentiments in the lyrics: "*how long must we sing this song – Sunday Bloody Sunday?*"

A wildly exciting "Electric Co." follows and the audience erupts again before the soothing balm of "A Sort Of Homecoming", dedicated by Bono "to the one I love": along with other members of the band's immediate families and close friends, she's there in the audience tonight to share in the promise "*I'll be there, I'll be there, tonight we will be as one tonight*" ... Bono *sings* the song, wrapping his vocal chords around the melody in longing, like a lover stretched on the rack of desire, for warmth, for friendship, for intimacy.

In contrast, there's nothing romantic about the urban metal of "Bad". "Everybody in Dublin isn't as lucky as us, joining a rock band and seeing the world", Bono announces. "In Dublin, where we come from, a lot of young people are unemployed. And to take away the pain a lot of them feel, they turn to heroin. This song is about a friend of mine whose girlfriend sold him enough heroin ... to kill him". After that harrowing excursion through the badlands of Dublin's smack addicts, the opening piano chords of "October" induce a feeling of fierce sadness ...

There's a hint of melancholy too on a superbly executed "New Year's Day" — the Edge switching smoothly from piano to guitar and back again throughout the song — before "Pride (In The Name Of Love)" uplifts and inspires in a big, heartfelt tribute to a man who has clearly made an enormous impression on Bono, Martin Luther King. It's a highly dramatic, moving end to a set that's been worked and honed 'till it sparkles and shines, diamond bright and twice as fine.

Throughout, Bono has revealed a highly-tuned empathy with the crowd. As of old — I remember it was a feature of one of the band's early McGonagles gigs — he inveigles a girl from the audience up to dance with him and she nearly collapses when he kisses her lips right up there in front of 20,000 people! Equally he handles a couple of stage invasions superbly, throwing his arm around the intruders and talking them quietly off the stage: one he rescues from a couple of slightly determined looking bouncers, before he's been aggressively manhandled. Now back for the first encore, he's asking if there's anyone in the audience who can play guitar. And it isn't a crude ploy to introduce Miami Steve Van Zandt (who as it happens *is* on the premises). This gawky youngster clambers over the security, onto the stage and Bono hands him his acoustic guitar. The message is that simple songs are often the most powerful: he teaches his protege the four chords and they launch into Bob Dylan's "Knockin' On Heaven's Door". The kid can't play for nuts (as it emerges when the band bring it right down later in the song) but he'll live forever on the shapes he throws: this truly is a magic moment, deceptively simple and risky in its way, but utterly memorable.

Another encore, and it's "Gloria" full throttle and full choral style. And finally, after prolonged and thunderous demands, flaming lighters held high for the umpteenth time, it's back again for "40".

And what a way to go! A football style chorus on the refrain "*How long, to sing this song*" and the band depart one by one, leaving just drummer Larry Mullen — who's been superb throughout — laying down a flawless beat for the audience to chant to. Larry keeps it going for a minute more, stops dead, waves to the sated fans and it's all over ...

In Madison Square Garden, 20,000 hearts beat as one. On stage the unforgettable fire and conviction of U-2's music had won them over, and won them totally. But it wasn't only a night of fire and brimstone — it was one of tenderness and emotion and inspiration.

After this triumph, their return to Ireland at Croke Park, after a two year absence on June 29th, should be some magnificent sort of homecoming for Adam Clayton, Larry Mullen, Bono and the Edge. I can't wait ..■

Niall Stokes
Vol 9 No. 7 April 26th, 1985

They complement each other well do Adam Clayton and Bono, respectively the bass player and singer with that promising Dublin beat combo called U-2.

Bono remains a charismatic individual, by turns passionate, funny, intense, confused, unpredictable — and always garrulous. Like most people, you might say — only more so. In conversation he's prone to leaping before he looks and is given to, on occasion, pulling some extraordinary — even embarrassing — analogy out of the hat. In the course of this interview he went even further and pulled down his trousers, revealing much to his (deliberately over-stated) shame, Calvin Klein underpants!

Bono, to understate it, is one of the few people in rock who can take the routine out of interviewing. Personally I'll always have plenty of time for him, though rarely enough tape.

By contrast, Adam Clayton exudes self-control, his contributions to the conversation being at all times considered, and concise. His, dare I say it, is a more sober voice than Bono's. Whereas the singer often verbalises what he's thinking as he's thinking it — damn the torpedoes and full speed ahead, as it were — Adam patiently bides his time, and when the moment is right, makes his point with the minimum of fuss and no melodramatics.

All of which might seem to confound Adam's public image as the band's rock 'n' roller — or at least that would have been the perception of him 'round about the time of U-2's first American tour.

"I was certainly out to enjoy what was on offer in that period," he says smiling. "Rock 'n' roll is such a legendary thing and to be a part of that is a great adrenalin boost. Certainly everytime we hit a city, I wanted to go and hang out in the clubs and absorb America and those sort of rock 'n' roll things. And I had some great times. You know, you'd meet people and they'd say "do you want to go to a party?" and it was great because it was like escaping from the tour. I mean we had been on that bloody bus for three months travelling all over America. You'd meet people and

The Homecoming

Back home in Ireland Bono and Adam talk to Liam Mackey

they'd invite you back to a house and it would just be a bunch of teenagers having a good time drinking beer and hollerin'. And it was great for me, and indeed for all the band – we had been working since we were 16 and we never had any money so we kind of missed out on that area of our youth. That sort of "bring your own" job, and settle in the corner with a six-pack. So it was great to get back to that and be in America, in a different place."

But as U-2's star rose within the business – with all the attendant pressures and temptations that entails – did you ever feel you were pushing the socialising too much? "I thought that I was kind of pushing it a bit, not with any kind of death wish but I thought, you know, "can I stay in there with the best of them and be a part of that?" Ultimately what happened was I became bored with it, because it is a fairly trivial world and I got it out of my system. I still have the odd night on the town, as everyone does but it's not a 24 hour, 7 day a week job."

One night on the town in Dublin, last year, saw the bass player end up on the front pages of the evening papers after an altercation with a guard – but I'd yet to hear him tell his side of the story.

"Ah, I'm not sure if my side needs to be stated really," he grins. "I think probably everyone knows the hyperbole of newspapers and that's all that really needs to be said. You know, it was a great headline but I wouldn't take too much notice."

The concert Irish fans will see in Croke Park will be very different to U-2's last outing in Dublin, two years ago in the Phoenix Park. That show was the culmination of the "War" tour which tour, Bono now says, went over the top.

"Yeah, it went over the top, over the wall, very badly offside, ran across a few fields, did a real obstacle course and nearly drowned in a river (laughs). I think I know that I have to accept responsibility for the drowning. I mean, I single-handedly nearly pulled the band under with me, because I was drowning."

Is that something you'd agree with Adam?

"I wouldn't be as harsh as Bono is. I think it was very much a case of getting into that twilight environment that you can get into, where you have been running down a tunnel for a very long time and your senses and reference points do change. That's what happened on that tour and after it, we needed a long time to recover before we could actually evaluate what we wanted to do and where we wanted to go."

"The Unforgettable Fire" album signposted, the new direction on record but in transferring it to stage, the band experienced teething problems, especially on the early shows in Australia.

"The whole feel of the stage set and stage show had to incorporate "The Unforgettable Fire", Adam recalls. "You know the "War" tour was very up and aggressive and loaded with ballads and a bit like a football crowd thing and you play up to that sort of approach. On "The Unforgettable Fire" tour we were trying to tone down the more sort of "oi" aspects of what we'd been doing (laughs). In a funny way, there was a time warp because the audiences that were coming had all seen "Under A Blood Red Sky", so there was some confusion I suppose in the crowd, as well as our confusion."

Their immediate instincts were to retreat from the theatricality of the "War" tour, to the point where Bono says, "our feet were nailed to the ground and the focus was interior as opposed to exterior. That was a great discipline, especially for me."

However as the tour moved on to Europe, the band realised they were in danger of simply switching formulae. "We had to throw it out," says Bono, "so things became very loose and it's got to the stage now

> "The "War" tour was very up and aggressive and loaded with ballads, a bit like a football crowd thing... On "The Unforgettable Fire" tour we were trying to tone down the more 'oi' aspect of what we'd been doing." — Adam

where nobody knows exactly what is going to happen on stage. It's got a bit on edge again.

" "The Unforgettable Fire" enabled us to get away from our live reputation in a way. We were able to say, look, we are making a record – it isn't a live show, it's music and it should be listened to . It is not something that should be watched. And that, in a way, is how the tour has settled in – in that the powerful moments of the set, are the musically powerful moments, as opposed to whatever is happening visually. The emphasis has moved away from the stage personalities. It has become unified·"

Adam encapsulates it thus: "The personality of the music, again, is the thing. We keep repeating that the music is much more important than the musician. Maybe in the "War" tour it was the other way 'round".

After that Phoenix Park concert of two years ago, Bono came off-stage and in the company of Bill Graham, pondered what had just happened. Triumphant as the show had been, he seemed to be concerned that had U-2 merely appeared on stage, they would have received a tumultuous response, as a matter of course. When I remind him of it, the singer is anxious to clarify what he

meant. "When I said that, I didn't say it in a way that suggested we have an unthinking audience. What I was saying was that the occasion was bigger than us. It was much bigger than the group U-2 and the people were applauding themselves on stage. I am coming to terms with this much more now. When there are 30,000 or 40,000 people or 50,000 people in a field or a car park or whatever, the sound system, however powerful, is incapable really of getting across your music so that the music people hear are the records they have at home. This is what they hear and those songs on those records are sound tracks to whatever they have been doing over the years, when they listened to that record. And they read their own life into the music, as I read my own life into other people's music. They are applauding themselves up on that stage. We are just ... I am humbled and honoured to be a part of that process but I am only a part of it."

A perceptive analysis — but could it contain the seeds of its own destruction? If the live performance is, for some of the audience, simply the records they hear at home, then is anything new happening at all? It was probably because of an awareness of the dangers of overfamiliarity that Bob Dylan, for one, chose to constantly re-invent his material in concert to the point where his shows, at their best, handed out a direct challenge to the audience. Adam: "I'm not sure that's valid nowadays. You see I think the climate is very different. People out there have actually spent their money on a ticket that they cannot afford and I don't think that they want to be educated. I think they actually want to have what they think they are buying, which is a couple of hours to get away from all the bullshit of how things are and how they had to save the money up in the first place. I think they just want a release."

Bono seizes on the word "release". "That's it. The thing even about that fight and Barry McGuigan's homecoming, is that all those people that lined the streets were not going to get the chance to have an in-depth conversation with the fighter. But everyone of them was in the ring and everytime he got a blow to the head they all got a blow to the head, and when he knocked that guy over, for everyone at home all over this depressed country, there was a release. And at that moment everyone stood up, husbands and wives and kids and others and there was something there, something was happening."

But if the concert is a release for the audience — for whom it might be a one-off experience — can it possibly also be a release for the band who've been touring for so long?

"Your body gets addicted to the adrenalin,"says Adam.
"Adrenalin — we are all addicted to it!" Bono agrees.

"You know the bigger and the better the performance, the worse we are the next day because I can't sleep after them, especially these out-door things. I can't sleep after them not for hours and hours and the only choice is to down a whole bottle of wine and this wears off after a while. And anyway, if you do that everynight of the week — you'll wind up looking like him!" (*points to Adam amid gales of laughter*).

Order restored, Bono continues. "It came to me on stage the other week, month, year, that this was the most familiar part of my life, this walking out on the carpet that covers our stage was much more familiar than the carpet in my front room — if I had a carpet in my front room! They say home is where the heart is but I think home is where the carpet is! Home is made up of familiar things, and I do not have a home. Home for me is Edge's keyboards; the amp box means a lot more to me than any light-stand or coloured television. You say that's touring but when I walk on stage it is like going home. It is actually like going home. The rest is work."

Eloquently stated, but playing devil's advocate one could argue that home-life often equals routine. Do U-2 have to combat the gig as routine?

Adam: "The only time it happens is when you are doing multiple dates in the same venue and then it is really difficult to walk back on that stage because it's almost like a residency in the Baggot Inn. But what you have to remember is that the audiences are different and you are not just up there doing it for them, you are up there because you need to do it as well. Because you have spent the whole day running around being interviewed or talking to people and that is your moment of peace and quiet. That is when nobody can talk to you. You have escaped once you get up there and if you come off stage not having done a good show, then the rest of the night is not yours, you don't feel good about it at all. So you have to be able to motivate yourself, you have to play the show of your life, up to that point."

The conversation turns to the current Irish music scene. U-2's emergence as a force on the homefront — apart all together from their later international breakthrough — was characterised by determination and imagination, as well as talent. In their shadow, a handful of bands look like they too could make giant strides, but many more have fallen by the wayside. Bono acknowledges the difficulties.

"I do sympathise with people who haven't got amplifiers, who haven't got gear, who haven't got rehearsal places. It's enough to make you want to tear your hair out, but I want to hear *the song* called "Tear Your Hair Out." It's not about musicians' *ability*, it's

Guitar men, Edge and Adam. Pic: Colm Henry

about sitting down and saying something that nobody else has said before. The other thing is this. I've learned spiritually, if you like, that the very things you need in your life are around you, at your feet but you don't see them. I didn't see them. I didn't know I was Irish till I left Ireland, I didn't realise that what was unique about U-2 was *us.* I was looking here, there and everywhere, and never looked under our feet, at the fact that we come from Dublin city — from Ireland — that there's a feeling here and you've got to feel that. Maybe it's rude and ignorant to talk about it especially as there are other people here, and I know them, who are living in bedsits where they haven't got the electricity to put on the radio and listen to Fanning to hear their demo tape being played."

On the subject of wealth, Bono looks back at U-2's early days as a period of richness — even though they didn't have much brass in pocket. "We were rich because of the friends we had, we were rich because we laughed at everyone and we laughed at each other. There was wealth in that laughter, a real wealth."

Eight years on, the band are experiencing another kind of wealth — the fiscal kind.

Bono: "We are making money for the first time this year — we are — but rock 'n' roll is not the goose that laid the golden egg. When we were on *Top Of The Pops* even for the second time we had to get the bus home. Because any money we had went into the band. And I'll tell you this, nobody would agree to the hours for the money, I mean no union would put up with it — for £30 a week."

But that was then and now U-2 *are* making money.

Adam: "It's given us an opportunity to actually *do* some of the things that we've always wanted to do. Like, build up a base here in terms of music. I was talking to Kieran Owens recently and he was saying "what you guys have done has been to give homebased Irish music some faith and confidence" and that's something that we want to keep developing and keep putting money into. I mean we're not gonna go around giving everyone £20,000 to make records or something because that's not the best way to use it. But I think it has given us the opportunity to be able to give something back to the community."

Bono: "It's like a footballer's income: the money you get is unbelievable really, it's such a lie that rock 'n' rollers live. I just think there must be very few people in the music business, in terms of artists, with money in the bank. Because they have it for a few years and it's gone then, and they have to live on it for the rest of their lives kind of thing. It's well out of proportion, the whole money thing. I think it would again be rude and ignorant, to say money isn't important to me because money is so important to a lot of people because they don't have it and I know I have it and I'm lucky and I thank God that I have money and I thank God that I can buy my old man a present or whatever.

"I mean we all have our personal philosophies, which would be very wrong to get into, about income. I'll tell you one thing: we could be a lot wealthier if we chose to be. That's in terms of decisions we have made over the years even as to what record company we have gone to, or in terms of the money in your hand and what to do with it and that is a dilemma each man must go through in the group himself."

At this point, it might be worth stating that enough of U-2's private life is already public — not everything they do or say can be for the record. Let's talk about the music ...

'd like to talk more about the music," Bono says, "I think because of the nature of the group U-2, people tend to talk *around* the group and *about* the group rather than the *music* in the group."

He has a point — and one which applies not only to U-2. Perhaps it's something to do with the changing nature — some would say degeneration — of rock criticism. In its supposed Golden Era of the late sixties and early seventies, rock criticism at least attempted to get inside the music and come out with some kind of revelation. Often it took the music, and itself too seriously and wound up courting pretension and looking plain silly, but, in general, there was a sense of interest, involvement and most importantly *concern* on the part of the critics, which seems to have largely disappeared.

In contrast, in 1985, supposedly informed debate about rock 'n' roll is too often less concerned with the music itself than it is with The Phenomenon, The Trend — in general, the cosmetic trappings of the thing. So getting away from that, let's hear you two talk about the music of this band U-2.

Adam: "I think "War" was very much the odd man out in the albums. "The Unforgettable Fire" harks back in some aspects to the innocence of "Boy" and the atmospherics of "October". I think that's its heritage, that's where we're coming from and "Under A Blood Red Sky" and "War" are pretty much partners in crime."

"Tapestry" is a word Adam and Bono use a lot when talking about "October" and "The Unforgettable Fire". But while there may be a lineage between the two, few would dispute that it was the latter album which really broke the back of the familiar U-2 sound. Their risk-taking on "The Unforgettable Fire" was not however without its pitfalls. "Elvis Presley And America", oblique to the point of incomprehensibility, is one track I couldn't — and still haven't — come to grips with.

Sitting it out, Larry and Bono. Pic: Colm Henry

Bono: "Dave Marsh, the *Rolling Stone* critic and biographer of Bruce Springsteen and The Who, really believes in U-2 and "Elvis Presley And America" was enough to make him want to smash his record player. Elvis Presley and America, two of the things he cared about more than anything else in the world and it made him so mad, he wrote off our record in absolute anger.

"I always enjoy the company of angry men and I met him six months later and he had been listening to "The Unforgettable Fire" every day, not because *he* put it on but because his 16 year old daughter had been putting it on. And it was no problem to her — she explained to him about "Elvis Presley And America".

"It was partly a reaction to the Albert Goldman book which tried to portray him as the archetypal r'n'r idiot, but the way he held the mike, the way he sang into the mike — this was a genius. But his decline just tore at me

> **"Writing songs scares the living daylights out of me. It's been a huge problem and I just run away I'm afraid. I have to accept responsibility for a lot of the chaos." — Bono**

and when I picked up the mike, it was a completely off the wall thing and I just began to sing.

"And I think it does evoke that decline, the stupor, the period when — if you've seen the clips of him — he forgets his words and fumbles."

At first Bono didn't want to release the track. Normally, because of the way he works, he would have developed and structured the original idea but both Eno and The Edge persuaded him to put it out, as raw as it was. In hindsight Bono agrees that it was the right thing to do, because he believes it allowed people a glimpse of "the original spark" of a U-2 song.

For different reasons, primarily personal, Bono was also hesitant about releasing "Promenade" but this listener is glad he changed his mind. It's a favourite of Adam Clayton's too as is "Indian Summer Sky" — "unusual for U-2 in that it has a lot of textures", he says — which epitomises the expansive, liberating quality of much of the music on "The Unforgettable Fire".

Bono: "That album was, in many ways, a contrast between bricks and mortar and music with the sky over its head.

"'Indian Summer Sky" was actually written in New York City and it had a sense of wanting to break through a city to an open place. Most of it was cinematic and very

fast — I'm getting away from that now, so I can talk about it."

The "Indian" in the title is a reference to the native American people, who were systematically wiped out during the nineteenth century.

Bono: "A lot of cities in America are built on civilizations long since buried by the American. A friend of mine, a wise man I know, spent a lot of time within the city — it was Toronto, so cool and so shiny — and he felt extremely troubled and torn in two. There had been a lot of massacres of Red Indian people in that area and he felt in some way as if there were troubled spirits still there. What I was trying to get across was a sense of a spirit trapped in a concrete jungle — something like that. Again these are just glimpses, these songs. A lot of the subject matter is very impressionistic."

Adam Clayton is Bono's sounding board in studio."He sits in on all the singing," the latter explains. "He's the only one usually, because he knows when I'm there and when I'm not there."

Adam: "Lyrical comprehension has never been particularly important to me. I go with my instincts and if Bono is singing and it doesn't sound right, then I'll consult him about it and say, "What exactly is going on — I can't figure this one out," But if the whole thing fits as an image, I don't listen to what he's singing, I listen to what I'm hearing in my head which is something completely different.

"I find that it's only after six months of touring it and listening to the record, that the songs start to get onto a different plane and speak to you and guide you in a funny way … I mean, you're getting a bit into Zen here (*laughter*), but it's like doing interviews, you're talking to people with different opinions in Europe or America or wherever and it's then you get into the inner truths of the song, which is not something Bono intended originally. His instincts were the same as everybody else's but gradually the sand and debris is swept away and the core is revealed."

Here again, U-2 find themselves at a point of departure. Bono has been thinking about his approach to writing, and has come up with the conclusion·that he hasn't started to "songwrite" yet.

"I have never tried to write this thing called a *song* that's played on radios all around the world," he elaborates, "that window cleaners hum, that people listen to in traffic jams. I never was interested in song: U-2 came about through a *sound*. Now I want to write a few songs. Most of the writing I've done — five years of it — has been more prose than song. I feel I must begin to come to terms with being a songwriter and actually start communicating on the first level as well as just on the third level. Springsteen is an expert at

communicating on the first level."

Bono will concede that U-2 have "a few songs" like "Pride" or "Sunday Bloody Sunday". But it's only now, he says, "for the first time in the history of the group that there are actually songs to be structured, songs to get into."

This is significant because up 'till now, it's been the music which has inspired the lyrics, with the latter often gelling only at the eleventh hour. Indeed, Bono admits that the delays in the completion of "The Unforgettable Fire" had much to do with problems he was encountering in lyric writing.

"Writing songs scares the living daylights out of me", he says. "It's been a huge problem and I just run away, I'm afraid. Again I have to accept responsibility for a lot of the chaos. I swore I wouldn't walk into it again and I did, I walked straight into it on the last album.

"It was a situation where we'd have the melody and the music. Now, I see the rhythm of words as being very important, and they build slowly up and often I don't think it's ready yet — though everyone else might think it is — but I can't let it go. That's why a lot of the songs tend to be sketches at the moment. "The Unforgettable Fire" — *"Carnival/Wheels fly and colours spin/through alcohol/red wine that punctures the skin/face to face in a dry and waterless place"* — it's a sketch, it builds up a picture but it's only a sketch. It doesn't really tell you anything. The music tells you about the mood of the person but it's not "a little ditty about Jack and Dianne"."

Precisely how a new, more disciplined approach to songwriting will affect U-2's music on their next album remains to be seen — even Bono is cautious at this point.

"The Edge always says records write themselves," he says. "I don't want to start writing it before I write it. We'll see."

U-2, unlike others in the music business, may not shore up the column inches with stories of rock 'n' roll madness and excess — but neither are they the pious puritans of certain popular mythology.

Why these young men have even recorded in the nude! Goodness! But it's true — to relieve the pressure during the difficult "Unforgettable Fire" sessions, all personnel connected with the making of the album took part in a naked day. "We got into gaffer art," Bono jokes, referring to the heavy-duty black tape with which they decorated their naked selves. According to Adam, co-producer Daniel Lanois "still bears the scars."

Bono: "Let's just say that he was using it as John The Baptist used a loincloth (*laughs*) anyway it was black and sticky and this brought laughter to us — but it brought tears to him when he had to take it off!"

A bit of harmless fun no doubt but the incident does remind us that there is a sense of humour within the U-2

The Edge pulls up to the bumper. Pic: Colm Henry.

collective which rarely transfers to vinyl. Bono demurs, saying there has been "a lot of humour in the music", but almost immediately concedes that it has been consigned to the b-sides of singles. Otherwise, I suggest, there does seem to have been a fairly unrelenting intensity and seriousness right through the band's recorded canon.

"I think the best thing to do at this stage is to say "blame it on me," says Bono. "It's a cliche at this stage — we don't take ourselves seriously but we do take the *music* very seriously. I think it's that the music that was important to me, is music that I listened to in a private place when I was on my own and that's the music you try to make — the music that made you, that inspired you in the first place."

Adam: "I think as we develop and move on, it's an aspect of the personality of the band that will come through. But we're only gradually coming to grips with what we do ourselves. That lightness is coming through, I think, in the live performance now. It's all to do with security, and what we've achieved so far and all that kind of stuff."

"We were *so* uptight." Bono adds, "That's what I sense, not seriousness. I don't listen to the records, the way Adam does — I hear them usually on the radio or something like that. But I played some of our records about six months ago and I sensed something there — I sensed real fear in me and a very tight and angry man — or boy/man as I was at the time.

"There's a certain period which the group went through which we still don't talk about — 2 or 3 years when we didn't even know if we wanted to be in a group. There was a lot of guilt over ... guilt over joy. It was winning out. And I can sense that in my singing.

"Now if you are uptight and angry you can compress the sound of your voice and so it goes higher or it gets squeakier. On "The Unforgettable Fire" I became a singer again. I allowed myself to loosen up and so the voice changes. People used to say, "I don't like this group, you know, pointing the finger" and I used to say, "We never point the finger at anyone but ourselves." But I could sense — when I listened back to "War" — I sensed for instance that there is real anger in that record and it could make you uncomfortable listening to it. So I could actually see, from another person's point of view how it could look like, you know, I'm preaching and it's a soap-box situation."

n, Atlanta, on their last US tour, the members of U-2 were invited to visit the Martin Luther King Centre by Coretta King — an event which Adam Clayton selects as being the moment in U-2's history which has made him most proud.

"The whole thing was not about patting each other on the back," he says, "it was just great to get

Bono under a dark grey sky. Pic: Colm Henry

Bono — all the world's a stage. Pic: Colm Henry

together and realise that we had similar feelings about things."

Bono remembers it vividly too, remembers being taken aback upon learning that the initials M.L.K. — the title of their elegiac tribute to the black leader on "The Unforgettable Fire" — were on Martin Luther King's briefcase the day he was assassinated. And as they entered the auditorium, the song that wafted out to meet them *was* "M.L.K.". Bono: "These people who were fighting for civil rights understood that music, more than they understood "Pride" which was rock 'n' roll music. They understood the tribute."

On the issue of black rights, Bono in particular has taken an unequivocal anti-apartheid stand in America, on at least one occasion joining a campus protest at one in the morning to express his solidarity. The black South African Bishop Tutu has been in touch with the band to thank them for their support, and while you get a sense that Bono is cautious about publicising such recognition, it's also clear that it meant a great deal to him.

But here, at home, have the band thought of getting involved with the Dunnes Stores strikers? "They have tickets for the concert," says Bono, "and we would like to meet them. It would be wrong for us to make a pronouncement because we don't know the issues involved — all I will say is that they are brave people in a city of cowards."

Not all U-2's memories of their last American tour are fond ones — there was an incident at a gig in Washington, for example, which could have had the gravest of consequences for both the band and their audience.

"Security men in every venue are briefed to lay-off, because if there are hands on our audience, we stop — we won't play," Bono explains. "When we walked out on stage in Maryland in Washington there was a huge line of security men with yellow t-shirts and "Crowd Control" printed on them, facing the audience, six inches from their faces, breathing on them, not allowing them to move out of their seats — it was like a Nazi rally rather than a rock 'n' roll concert.

"I asked the crowd, "Look if you want to let go, don't let these people hold onto you." And maybe it was a mistake in hindsight because they let go and the place exploded. They pushed these securitymen — all 20 of them — out and then they sent in *more* security. A riot broke out and we had to stop the concert. At this stage the riot police were brought in.

"I was just about to say something when Paul McGuinness just turned me 'round and said "look, this is a situation that's becoming a confrontation and if you open your mouth once more the security people are going to take control of the building and turn the power

Smiles all 'round. Pic: Colm Henry

off." He advised me not to say anything and I didn't."

However, when U-2 had finished a shortened set and the pandemonium had died down, it quickly dawned that the police had plenty to say to Bono — and to Paul McGuinness and stage manager Steve Iredale. They wanted to arrest all three on charges of incitement to riot.

Bono: "We realised that the headlines "U-2 Riot, Arrest" would go around America for the rest of the tour. We were going to be monitored, people would not be able to move out of their seats, we were going to be marched off to the police station — people wouldn't be allowed to go to the concerts because all people would see was "U-2 Riot!" "U-2 Riot!"

Backstage negotiations were entered into with the relevant authorities and Bono was told "we don't know where you come from but where we come from, we take these things *very* seriously."

Bono: "So I told the Fire Chief, "All I can say is these people pay our wages and they pay your wages and they pay the Mayor's who works over you and they deserve respect from us and from you!" I did this speech, a briliant speech and he says "Boy, you're not to blame, *they're* to blame — and he points at McGuinness and Steve and I said "Oh no!" (*laughs*).

Eventually, after further discussion, tour manager Steve Iredale, who had signed a contract which contained a clause forbidding the band to encourage people to leave their seats, was arrested and subsequently freed on bail. The U-2 camp intend to challenge his arrest, for as Bono quips: "Steve is not guilty — free Steve!"

Months on, the band may be able to look back and see some humour in the situation, but the seriousness of the Maryland incident was not lost on them and has led to a policy, that in Bono's words means "U-2 will not walk on to a stage in a hostile environment."

In practical terms, this has meant having to switch venues in a number of cities in the States. As Adam puts it: "The problem is that we're passing through but these people are still there and if there is a hall with this sort of problem we will just play somewhere else and that's that."

But of bad experiences come lessons that are well learned and as Croke Park approaches, the band are striving to ensure, that as at Slane for Springsteen, all will go well on the day.

"What U-2 are about is the very opposite of what these people are about," says Bono, "and Jim Aiken has guaranteed me personally that the people who are working on security in Croke Park will be well-briefed and will treat the people in the audience well.

"I hope and pray that Croke Park will be just the most peaceful and uplifting event. I just hope that people will look after each other in the crowd and up-front if a crush develops. And I hope that goes from the people right at the front to the back, because the concert will be only as good as the people want it to be. That is the way I look at it.

"And the people who are walking around on the periphery looking at it, if you like, through eye-glasses, will miss out on what the U-2 concert is about — involvement." ■

Liam Mackey
Vol 9 No. 12 July 5th, 1985

Bono and friends. Pic: Colm Henry

142

Stories of Boys

The inside story on the early years by Jackie Hayden.

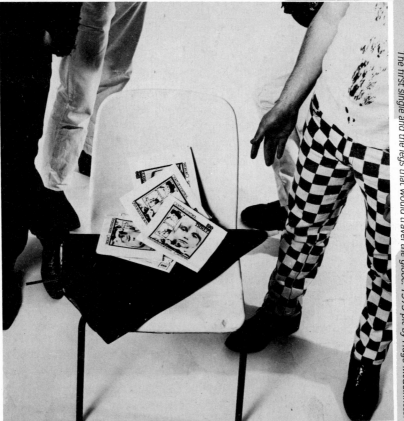

The first single and the legs that would travel the globe. 1979 pic by Hugo McGuinness.

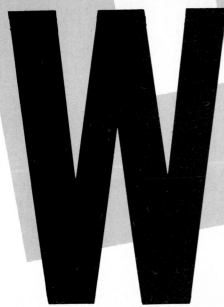

Working in record marketing in Ireland in the late 70's offered, amongst many dubious pleasures, the opportunity to sit in judgement on panels for talent competitions. I say dubious because although a splendid time could be had at someone else's expense (usually my employers, CBS) listening to a lot of good and a lot of bad music, it was a dangerous vocation at the best of times.

In fact, I eventually decided that I didn't have the calling for it after adjudicating a talent competition in the now defunct Talk Of The Town in Aston Quay, Dublin. After the results had been announced, the parents of a losing seven-piece accordion band, tackled fellow judge RTE DJ Larry Gogan and myself about our credentials. There is a saying, that a gentleman is someone who knows how to play an accordion, but doesn't. These were no gentlemen!

Proving that the line between cowardice and pacifism is almost invisible, Larry slipped out the back leaving me to explain matters to fourteen disgruntled parents. Eventually the police had to be called and I was escorted, B.P. Fallon style, to my car.

Not that there hadn't been good times too. In particular I remember sitting on the panel of a folk competition in Tralee as part of the Rose of Tralee Festival. The jury were comfortably ensconced in a bank

143

office overlooking the town square, where the various groups played to a large crowd from a stage, positioned so that we, the jury, could see the acts, but fortunately they couldn't see us.

With typical Kerry hospitality, the room was heavily stocked with a variety of drinks, and after a while more attention was being paid by the panel to the comparative merits of the alcohol on offer, than to the skills of the performers. By about the fifth act, most of the panel were either drunk or asleep and I think the final decision was made by the bank's overnight security man.

After all that, I don't know how I allowed myself to be talked into sitting on the panel for a Limerick Civic Week pop/rock competition on St. Patrick's Day 1978, but I did. Maybe I just fancied a few days out of Dublin or perhaps I thought fellow panellist Billy Wall from RTE Radio, would offer better protection than Larry Gogan had. Either way, there was something significant at stake this time — the winning act would get the chance to audition for the CBS label.

Three days later, "Out Of Control" became the biggest selling twelve inch record ever in Ireland. Radio 2 DJ's right across the board got behind it and soon all 1,000 limited edition pressings were sold.

Not that many of the performers seemed to care, mind. After listening to about twelve appalling acts, I began to wish that the lads in Tralee had organised this one. In all I think we listened to about thirty-eights acts, out of which only a couple had something to offer.

One was a band called East Coast Angels, who had already enjoyed some publicity in the Sunday World and were an amalgam of Gary Glitter, Slade, Mott The Hoople and Magic. Another band to impress contained four young looking kids from Dublin. They called themselves U-2.

While the overall acoustics and sound system worked against many of the bands, U-2 exuded a determination to play and perform despite the technical problems. They did three numbers, including one in Irish, possibly an early incarnation of An Cat Dubh.

I remember Bono impressing me most, with a superbly confident stage presence, even though a tired throat produced overtones of Rod Stewart. I remember his "I'm not moving, feet apart" stance, which has become legendary, and he wore a tight grey polo-neck sweater. He was neat. The rest of the band looked serious and went about their respective jobs in a workmanlike fashion. They knew they were good and both Billy Wall and myself liked them instantly.

Later that evening the chosen finalists had to return to the same hall to perform again, this time in front of an audience. From discussions I had with Billy Wall, it seemed almost certain that either the East Coast Angels or U-2 would win out, unless some of the other acts pulled some miracle from a yet-invisible hat. We also agreed that the overall standard had been disturbingly bad.

We could not understand this, since there was a top prize of £500 (not bad in 1978) plus the remote possibility of joining ABBA, Dylan, Springsteen and Geraldine Brannigan in the CBS camp.

Finally, the moment of truth arrived and when the points were added up, U-2 were the outright winners. Then with an act of cowardice reminiscent of Larry Gogan, Billy Wall suggested I should make the announcement and hand over the prize. Thanks Billy!

Being quite aware that a Dublin man presenting a prize to a Dublin band on a Limerick stage might not be the most popular man in town, I indulged in a spot of emergency thinking as I made my way to the stage.

I congratulated U2, made an unpopular reference to the obvious lack of rehearsal by some of the acts, and expressed the hope that maybe U-2 might someday achieve even some measure of the success enjoyed by that great local Limerick act Reform. That last reference was a master stroke, and it was the nearest I ever got to a standing ovation in my life!

A few weeks later U-2 were booked into Keystone Studios in Dublin for their audition to fulfil the agreement CBS had made with the Limerick Civic Week Committee. Some of the band have since been understandably critical of aspects of that session. However, I don't think that they fully understood that the practical intention was to record about eight or ten numbers live, so that CBS could assess the band's repertoire in a way that would not be possible if we'd spent too much time concentrating on just two or three songs. After all, it was their first recording date, they were extremely nervous and no one was expecting miracles. And for the record: subsequent claims by Bono that the band were not allowed into the control room are pure fantasy. (Sorry, Bono).

Anyway the evening ended quite abruptly when Larry Mullen's Dad arrived to take an indignant Larry home. Larry was only fifteen at the time and his Dad felt that school next morning was far more important than this recording session.

The end product from that session was unimpressive

Main pic Bono in 1981 (Colm Henry) and inset the boy in 1978 (Bernard Farrell).

Paul McGuinness and Adam Clayton in 1978. Pic: Bernard Farrell.

of itself, but nevertheless I was getting to like the material and the band more and more. U-2 had a particular way of concentrating on the job in hand, which I found lacking in most Irish bands at the time, although I recall their overall sound was not helped by the tuning problems Dave Edge had with his guitar.

Some weeks after this session, Adam Clayton and Paul Hewson (now Bono to you and me) called to my office. They were looking for a CBS recording deal. While nobody else at CBS Ireland was remotely interested in the band, I was keen for a number of reasons to keep up the contact, even though I thought Adam Clayton a little too demanding for my liking! Since they had no manager at the time, I sent Adam a copy of a standard CBS Ireland contract for them to consider.

At a further meeting in my office, Adam explained the band's position. "We don't want to sign this particular contract, there are quite a few things we don't like about it, and since we are all so young, we think we can wait a while before committing ourselves". I explained that the situation was not negotiable, that at that time CBS UK were of the opinion that CBS Ireland should not be signing acts at all, and that was that.

Before leaving the office, Adam asked me, "If we don't sign with CBS now, will that mean that you won't want to have anything further to do with us?"

I told him, no, I was more than happy to keep in touch with the band and I wasn't going to take their refusal to sign personally. What many people don't realise is that individuals in my position gain little and lose nothing, whether record companies sign bands or not.

In the weeks that followed, I had several more meetings with the band and got to know a lot about them. Larry Mullen appeared to be the only one who could actually read music, which probably stemmed from his father being a keen jazz enthusiast. They also joked about the fact that it was originally Larry's band, explaining that when Larry had asked Bono to join, the singer had refused. Then when they did get together at a later date Bono's personality was so dominant that the Larry Mullen Band temporarily became the Bono Hewson Band.

I also learned that their name had been suggested by Steve Rapid, whom I knew from the Radiators From Space. During one of these discussions it was suggested that maybe I should take over the management of the band, but this was an area of the music industry in which I had little interest. Even at that early stage some of the band's later heavily-publicised interest in politics and social issues came through in conversation. I can recall on at least one occasion having to improvise a diplomatic soft-shoe shuffle in response to their misgivings about CBS' involvement with the singer Geraldine Brannigan whose visits to South Africa they saw as support for that country's evil apartheid regime.

Some time later I had a telephone call from Paul McGuinness who informed me that he was now managing U-2 and wanted to meet me. I was already slightly familiar with Paul from his involvement with the Irish folk rock group Spud, and his championing of the American singer songwriter Thom Moore, who was then resident in Ireland. When Paul and I met it was obvious that we shared a natural enthusiasm for U-2, both as people and as musicians.

I continued to go to see U-2 as often as I could, and I can remember some really good gigs at the Project Arts Centre, The Baggot Inn and the now legendary Saturday afternoon gigs at the Dandelion Market of St. Stephen's Green. I remember songs like "Trevor", "Cartoon World" and "Jack In The Box", which impressed me enormously. But I always maintained to Paul McGuinness that the band would need a very sympathetic producer to transfer the excitement they created at a live gig, on to tape. Paul later played me a demo produced by Barry Devlin, (formerly of Horslips), which was certainly infinitely better than the audition tape I had produced. There were three songs on Barry's session, "Street Missions", "Shadows In Tall Trees", and "The Fool". However, much as I liked these new recordings, I still felt that there was a major gap to be bridged between U-2 live and U-2 in a recording studio.

Around this time I bumped into Bill Graham of Hot Press, at a gig in the Project Arts Centre at which U-2 were supporting a Dublin band called The Gamblers. Bill was equally enthusiastic about U-2's future, and was one of their earliest and most fervent media supporters. (Indeed, it emerged that it was Bill who had introduced the band to Paul McGuinness). Our support was vindicated as U-2 emerged as the heroes of a special twenty four hour marathon gig at the Project Arts called Dark Space, at which a number of Northern and UK bands played.

Unfortunately, my championing of U-2 was not exactly scoring points for me within CBS, where the tradition in Ireland had been to favour recording MOR acts like Geraldine Brannigan, Roly Daniels, Twink and Alma Carroll. As you can imagine, U-2 did not fit comfortably into that roster and it was also openly expressed to me, that my efforts could better be spent promoting some more sales of Leonard Cohen records.

My main argument for U-2 was based not just on the quality of their material and what I saw as their obvious commercial potential — I was also keen that CBS should pick up a major Irish international act. Horslips, Chris de Burgh, Rory Gallagher and the Boomtown Rats had all been missed out on by CBS UK, before going on to bigger things. I also argued that there was a real danger that CBS as a major international company might even be seen to be anti-Irish.

Eventually, as a result of the sterling efforts of Paul McGuinness, we were able to persuade CBS to send Nicky Graham from their London A & R division, over to hear U-2 playing live. Nicky was sufficiently impressed to keep up a dialogue with Paul and he even came back again to a specially arranged private performance one lunchtime at McGonagles.

I remember discussing the songs with him afterwards and "Cartoon World" was one he fancied as a single. Although he may not have admitted it to Paul McGuinness lest he weaken his negotiating position, I knew Nicky Graham was keen to sign U-2 to CBS UK.

On the local scene the buzz about U-2 was reaching fever pitch and I knew that some other companies were sniffing around, encouraged no doubt by Paul McGuinness. Eventually it was agreed that CBS would send Chas de Whalley over to Windmill Studios to record some serious demos. I felt we were getting somewhere at last.

When I heard the demos of "Boy Girl", "Stories For Boys", and "Out Of Control", I was astounded.. In fact to this day the opening bars of "Out Of Control" are as spine-tinglingly exciting as they were then. A couple of days later I saw the band play another amazing gig at the Dandelion Market. Something was definitely happening.

During the next week I spoke to more CBS people trying to convince them that this was a real buzz and not just hype. I then began to hear rumblings that certain members of the CBS UK hierarchy felt that U-2 could be a worthwhile band, but that they needed a better drummer. This was a laughable idea since Larry Mullen was undoubtedly the most accomplished individual musician in the band at the time and Nicky Graham had already expressed to me his view, that any producer working with U-2 would have one simple problem: persuading Larry to play within himself rather than playing to the limits of his capabilities.

It was around that time that I obviously did something wrong with my mouth, because I had a call from a CBS UK executive, telling me more or less to mind my own business and that the CBS A & R division could "Take care of U-2 and Paul McGuinness."

Then I had a shattering phone call from CBS in London. "We're passing on U-2", they said. I couldn't believe it. Apparently at a CBS A & R meeting at which various tapes were played, the U2/Chas de Whalley demo was given an airing. The legend has it that CBS UK Chairman, Maurice Oberstein, demanded to know if U-2 would make money for CBS within a year. An A & R man, probably Nicky Graham, argued that U-2 would probably take two/three years to really develop, Oberstein repeated his question and when Graham answered "no ... but" the die was cast.

Back in Dublin an urgently arranged meeting with Paul McGuinness took place. We discussed the new situation. We talked about the Irish market and the role it might play in launching U-2 onto the international scene. We talked about the various marketing ploys currently being used in the UK, including multi-coloured discs, see-through vinyl, oddly-shaped discs, twelve-inchers, the lot. I said that if the U-2 release in Ireland was going to work, it would have to be seen to be anything but another Irish single by another Irish rock band destined for the bargain bins.

At a further meeting I suggested that we should put out a three track twelve inch limited edition of one

Pic: Eamonn O'Dwyer

Jackie Hayden in his CBS office Dublin, 1979, with copies of the debut single.

1981. Adam Clayton beats the new wave. Pic: Colm Henry

thousand copies, with each record individually numbered. I argued that as far as we knew the idea of numbering a limited edition had not been done in the UK. Paul bought that one, and added his own suggestion: that we should have a simultaneous release of a seven inch version of the same tracks in a picture sleeve, designed by Steve Rapid.

A meeting was set up with David Duke, General Manager of CBS Ireland, to work out a deal for signing U-2 to CBS for Ireland only. In the meantime I went to London and spoke to Nicky Graham. I argued that since CBS UK had paid for the three track demos and were no longer interested, could they not give those tapes to CBS Ireland for us to release. He checked and the relevant authority in CBS UK said, "Yes".

Paul and I also agreed that there would be two key elements in our promotional strategy. One was Hot Press and the other was Dave Fanning. At that time Hot Press was becoming an increasingly important factor in communicating to the rapidly growing rock market, and Dave Fanning with his rock show on the fledgling Radio 2 was equally critical. Fortunately, my relationship with Dave and with Niall Stokes, the editor of Hot Press, had been positive and amicable. Different proposals were put to each. We asked Dave if he would play all three tracks of the proposed single and ask his listeners to choose what should be the A-side. Separately Paul and myself spoke to Niall Stokes, editor of Hot Press. We were asking for him to put U-2 on the cover with an interview inside. This was unheard of. A band with no recording history had never featured on a Hot Press cover. With characteristic immodesty I argued

148

When stock arrived from the local pressing factory, I personally set about numbering each individual copy from 1 to 1,000. In the process I contacted some of the people I knew in the most rock orientated record shops and used the special numbering ploy to extract orders from them. For example, Pat Egan was at first reluctant to take a risk on a large quantity but when he was promised numbers one to twenty-five he agreed to take them. Similarly, other shops got special numbers, such as 500 and 999.

Three days later, "Out Of Control" became the biggest selling twelve inch record ever in Ireland. Radio 2 DJ's right across the board got behind it and soon all 1,000 limited edition pressings were sold and the seven inch was beginning to sell in high quantities. Obsessed with the proof that I had been right all along, I telexed CBS London to the effect that they should reconsider their decision to pass on U-2. I don't recall the exact wording of the telex , but Paul McGuinness claims to have a copy of it "in safe keeping". I never got a reply.

Soon after the success of the single, U-2 signed to Island Records, to whom they are still contracted, although CBS still retain the group's records for Ireland only.

Not that it should be assumed that all was forever sweetness and light between the band and CBS. There were numerous flashes of conflict between Paul McGuinness and David Duke of CBS.

At one point CBS Ireland considered dumping the band. The incident which brought things to a head occurred after I'd left CBS in 1980. Apparently the band were quoted in an interview with a now-defunct Irish magazine as feeling that CBS were not getting them enough publicity — the irony was that the interview had been arranged by CBS staffer Mary Duane who had taken over some of my responsibilites after I left. Besides, it was the kind of negative publicity that David Duke, CBS MD at the time, wanted like a hole in the head.

Fortunately, common sense prevailed and CBS have continued to issue U-2's material in Ireland right up the present day — a substantial coup in that the local company picked up a major international act, having invested very little money to begin with: that investment must by now have been repaid a hundred fold.

For their part what CBS did do was to give U-2 an initial footing on the ladder that eventually led to their international success. Of that everyone who was involved in the company at the time can still feel justifiably proud. ■

Jackie Hayden

Vol 9 No. 13 June 20th, 1985

that since some people were prepared to lay their necks on the line for U-2, those people deserved Hot Press support. As it was, critical support for U2 among the writers of Hot Press was already well-established at this point. Niall Stokes checked with Bill Graham and spoke to others, before phoning back to confirm: we had lift-off!

To further ensure that this record should be regarded as something very different, a special listening session was set up in Windmill Lane, where the entire CBS staff met the individual members of the band and heard the tracks for the first time. Since it was normal practice in the record industry to ignore sales staff and stores staff, the psychological benefit of this approach was enormous — everyone felt that they were part of the plan and enthusiasm ran high.

All Ireland Champions!

U-2 bring it all back home to Croke Park.

IT WAS the opening night of the Dublin Street Carnival — an occasion for the people of Dublin to feel a sense of pride and unity, so often denied them in a sprawling city of architectural devastation and rampant unemployment.

That was the buoyant feeling of good-will which characterised the gathering in the Grapevine Arts Centre. And at the centre of it were U-2, sponsors of the Unforgettable Fire exhibition which was opening there, the night before the band's Croke Park megabash. On the wall, images of man's terrible capacity for destruction offered a chilling reminder of the darker forces occasions like this are made to exorcise. Bodies burnt, broken, bruised and rotting: first-hand accounts of the scenes of appalling devastation visited on Hiroshima and Nagasaki in the final throes of the Second World War.

Downstairs, Martin Luther King's magnificently courageous career as a Civil Rights activist was celebrated, down to the final spread from Life magazine. Malcolm X swam in a pool of red — his own blood. The message of U-2's music — that we must wrestle with the demons of violence and hatred and aggression and that we must win. Peacefully.

It's a message that can hardly be lost on the people of Dublin in 1985. There is a need now for an infusion of generosity, comradeship, optimism and love. The impact of recklessness and ruthlessness on the city can be exaggerated — but it could become a tidal flood if legislators and the forces of law and order continue in their apparent policy of upping the *ante*. The Unforgettable Fire exhibition, U-2's music, the Dublin Street Carnival, in their different ways, are about giving that necessary infusion.

Through the "Unforgettable Fire" exhibition, U-2 have found a way to give something back to the city that brought them together. It was a symbol of their pride in their place of birth, it's people, and their commitment to it — graciously acknowledged by the Lord Mayor Michael O'Halloran and the City Manager Frank McFeeley on the night. Looking at the images, hearing the speeches, feeling the rising tide of genuine goodwill, you could truly believe it. Tomorrow Croke Park would explode with the righteous sound of 55,000 cheering fans and we could say for sure: The Jacks are back! ...

———————————●———————————

Well, this is only a stone's throw from the Dandelion Market, and Mount Temple up the road, and yet it's a million miles, and the people who crammed the pitch and the stands have been gathering along the way. U-2 had a homecoming and this was the party. The band and the audience had things to say to each other, a ritual dialogue of welcome and congratulations, a people's benediction and salute to the conquering heroes — like they had to Barry McGuigan before — and the band in turn, back from their voyages and triumphs came to invoke the spirit, the rhythm, the occasion, the soul and the heartscapes of home and reunion.

So this was more than a gig. It was the closing of another circle. It was a renewal. Above all else it was an affirmation and a communion. I am U, you are 2, and we are all (U)2gether — in Croke Park, gawd bless the bishop's bones.

They were there at half-eight on the dot. A new precedent has been established this year by Bruce and U-2 — thou shalt begin on time. Fittingly it was with "11 O'Clock Tick Tock" and "I Will Follow" blasting, no *surging* from the speakers. A forest of fists, participation, concentration.

The transition to the giant gig has been easy for U-2. Their music has always derived its strength from inclusiveness and participation. Bono sings and calls to the group, the crowd, the plural, unlike Springsteen, whose move to the great outdoors has been more fragile because of the intimacy of his relationship with his hearers, who listen as a collective of individuals.

Moreover, they have incorporated the more atmospherically and lyrically complex "Unforgettable Fire" material into the set with ease. Their performance now is one of assurance and mastery — dare one say maturity.

Big stages are made for Bono, his exuberance and mobility finding its natural extension in catwalks and large open spaces. But again one sensed pacing — he didn't gibbon around the scaffolding — and throughout their performance the band as a whole never overkilled, they restrained themselves to whatever was right, for the moment. They never blew it.

The fourth song, "MLK" brought the first shiver up the spine. "*If the Thundercloud passes rain, let it rain*" and it looked for a time as though it might. "*So let it be*".

The guitar band at Croke Park. Pic: Colm Henry.

Ah yes. Resignation, acceptance.

The second macroshiver came from "Sunday Bloody Sunday", not just for the crowd's justifiable enthusiasm for the song's sentiments, their participation in the performance and the power of their commitment. No, there was more to this one — there were ghosts about, because the original Bloody Sunday, happened there in Croke Park, when the Black and Tans gunned down fourteen people, fans and players, at a football match on November 21st 1920, in reprisal for the assassination of eleven British intelligence officers and soldiers, under the direction of a member of Fine Gael's pantheon, Michael Collins. These assassinations were a brilliant, ruthless revolutionary achievement . . .or a dastardly loathsome, terrorist outrage.

Take your pick. Fine Gael have, and they've cut the past, and the truth, to suit the needs of the present. In modern Ireland, of course, they're far from alone, but that's another story. One way or another, the Tans had their revenge and as ever, then as well as now, it was the innocents who were to suffer. No wonder the ghosts sang along, no wonder the stands reverberated to "Sunday Bloody Sunday" with such special, extraordinary empathy. How long must we sing this song, indeed.

But the most extraordinary moment came with "Pride (In The Name Of Love)". This was ...

Are there words for it? Beyond extraordinary. Only believeable because it happened with all those witnesses!! All those fists in parallels in the air, and every fucking voice in the cauldron singing the chorus, a sound unlike any other, audible in Howth, Finglas, Ballyfermot and Dun Laoghaire, a truly awe-inspiring communion.

Sun Ra has a theory that if every musician on earth were to play a C7 that the world would shift on its axis, that it would become a more balanced and better place. Well that is the kind of force that was unleashed. Stunning.

It was, perhaps, the moment where the gig passed into folk memory! The rest of the encores took the concert to its natural conclusion, but that was the climax. They followed it with Bruce Springsteen's "My Hometown", probably not much rehearsed, and showing in an endearingly innocent series of fluffed chords how far U2 are from the classic mould of rock band, Larry Mullen excepted.

Larry (*squeal!!*) it was who had the last word from the band at the end of "40", as he drummed away after the others had, one by one left the stage, a stark and perfect conclusion ... but the crowd had their comeback, as they continued the song out into the streets, around the stadium, filtering away towards the city centre and integrating with the garrulous mayhem of the carnival. ■

Niall Stokes and Dermot Stokes
Vol 9 No. 13, July 18th, 1985.

Reeling in the Years

A U2 miscellany from the pages of Hot Press 1978-85.

NEWLY-FORMED Dublin New Wave band U-2 scored a blow for rock 'n' roll when they won the top prize of £500 in a group contest co-sponsored by the *Evening Presss* and *Harp Lager* held recently during the Civic Week in Limerick. That's what you call getting the breaks ...

U-2's first ever mention in Hot Press, Vol 1 No. 21, March 30th 1978.

●

U-2 mayn't be out of school yet but they're certainly showing the suss in managing their affairs which many older bands haven't yet learned ...

Vol 1 No. 22 April 13th 1978.

●

They were fun to dance to, but the School Kids have more than a few wrinkles to iron out before they'll leave a lasting impression.

On the other hand, U-2 have only one big problem, conquering the 'fast-is-good' fallacy that plagues them now. Already possessed of a fine rhythm section, a tangible identity, and a promising vocalist, U-2 managed to negate the impact of their originals simply by playing too fast. What could well have been very clever songs sounded unintelligible and indistinguishable.

A glimmer of U-2's direction may be gleaned from the inclusion of Wire's "Mannequin" in their set, and if U2 can slow down long enough to be heard, they could step to the fore of the Dublin music scene.

Karl Tsigdinos
Vol 2 No 1. June 8th 1978.

●

It's as well Revolver have finally found themselves with competition like U-2 on the up and up. With a passionate lead singer who's not one to ape other's microphone poses and a guitarist who supplies a mild metal additive, U-2 are impressive contenders with the appetite and talent to improve beyond their already creditable status.

Standing apart from this year's new bands in their suss and willingness to learn that will soon end any technical faults, U-2 profit from the fact that they've an identity that needs little alteration. Revolver recovered in time but they had better not stand still. U-2 are ready to pass everyone out.

Oh and both bands slew last week's British import, Advertising. Guaranteed Irish, guaranteed quality.

Bill Graham
Vol 2 No. 6. August 17th 1978

Pic: James Mahon.

U-2: (Trinity Buttery and McGonagles Matinee).

IT'S NO SECRET at headquarters that I have a special spot for U-2. Indeed I've no hesitation in rating them the best unrecorded band in Ireland and one whose potential is still barely tapped.

Unfortunately, circumstances weren't the best for this review. Production of our yearbook meant that their two recent McGonagles gigs, the first for the Hot Press/McGonagles party itself, the second on the third day of this New Year passed without praise in print. They were simply the most exhilarating performances by a local band I've witnessed in the last twelve months.

Last Saturday week, U-2 played twice. The matinee was at McGonagles, an enterprising foray to capture the teen audience

barred by licensing laws and late night opening.

Unprofessionally, my clock stopped so I lost an hour, only appearing to catch the last four numbers. Neither I nor U-2 were happy with the sound but the band did succeed in their primary aim of attracting and impressing a sizeable underage contingent. They return there this weekend.

(Memo to McGonagles: because these customers aren't winedrinkers, extra effort must be made to aid the atmosphere).

The later date was two hundred yards down the road in Trinity but the late arrival of the hired equipment and a hurried sound-check weren't the best preparation. U-2 were solace for the bewildered, even if

their set slumped slightly in the final third, before a racing version of "Street Mission". So if the band were scrambling, it's indicative of their growth that an average set nonetheless promotes their merits rather than exposing their failings.

...am, Bono and The Edge with Virgin Prune Guggi

Partially, it's due to Paul Hewson. Undoubtedly, the best front-man since Geldof, he's a powerfully-charged battery of energy, and utterly unignorable. His enthusiasm is such that even a potentially pessimistic song like "Concentration Cramp" doesn't flounder in grim negativity, he and the band trampling underfoot all those confining restrictions of school-days.

Furthermore, except for one purloined Kinks riff, U-2 owe no obvious debts to earlier styles. Their songs are uniquely their own, vibrant celebrations that are both direct in impact yet not so simple in style. It's U-2's most enduring asset that they've taken only the ideals of the new wave, but not its licks, so that while their songs retain pop vivacity, their structures stretch towards more complex forms. They are already their own category.

So many estimates of local bands end with double-edged compliments, ifs, buts and lukewarm qualifications. U-2 belong to a whole other league.

Bill Graham
Vol 2 No. 17. February 8 1979.

●

But perhaps the most fascinating battle of all came in the most promising band category, where The Bogey Boys finally won through — a performance which will undoubtedly have been helped by their maximum T.V. exposure just prior to the event. Again, the New Wave bands may well have suffered from a more frag-

U2 at Wembley for Live-Aid, Saturday July 13th, 1985.

Pic: Mark Classon

mented vote with The Undertones, The Vipers, and Berlin all very close and U-2, DC Nien and The Virgin Prunes also polling well. What's most clear however is that there's a vast pool of impressive talent there.

Hot Press Readers Poll
Vol 2 No 18. February 22nd 1979.

●

"Death Race 2,000" had passed its half-way mark when U-2 took the stage to the hearty applause of the dedicated followers of fashion who had forgotten to bring sleeping bags. And the band's rock 'n' roll breakfast tasted just fine.

With perfect posturing and dynamic delivery, Paul Hewson, straining every muscle and pulling the band forward, was always arresting. While they were always confident and competent Dave Evans (gtr.) and Adam Clayton (Bass), belied the intermittent tendency to drag the music into the clutches of the age-old malaise of heavy metal sludge, especially on the shadily atmospheric "Shadows and Tall Trees". The sound was crisp enough, but Tayto it ain't. Yet on numbers like "Cartoon World" and "Another Time, Another Place" they showed enough bravado and intelligence to convince anyone that this young band has hair on its chest. "Street Missions" was great. Their encore "Glad To See You Go" was energetic but it suffered slightly from its slower-than-Ramones pace. Not to worry. Their own numbers and enthusiasm will see them through.

Radio 2's leading rock DJ Dave Fanning, reviewing the Dark Space 24-hour event in the Project Arts Centre. Vol 2 No. 18 February 22nd 1979.

In London for the "Sense of Ireland" festival 1980 (l to r): Gavin of the Virgin Prunes, Bono of U2, Guggi of The Virgin Prunes, Brian Freeze of Berlin, Damian Gunn of D.C. Nein and John Borrowman of The Atrix. Pic: Colm Henry.

Boys will be boys. Early pic by Patrick Brocklebank.

U2: Three (CBS)
1.) "Out of Control" – the paradox being that the single itself is very tightly controlled, almost to the point of suffocation. The vocals are so far back in the mix that some of the coiled energy implicit in the music is dissipated in trying to catch what's going on. 2.) "Stories for Boys" is by far my favourite – it's unbelievably fast, but not simply to impress. The lyrics work better that way, coinciding in feeling with the natural adrenalin rush of the rest of the song. 3.) "Boy/Girl" is well thought out, tight and effective: a good song, but not as spontaneous as "Stories".

If DJ's pick up on "Stories", the band should have a major and a thoroughly deserved hit. But why is the weakest track the A side?

U-2's first Irish single, reviewed by Sandy Harsch Vol. 3 No. 9 October 12th 1979.

●

U-2 are extending operations in London during the first half of December. Already

the band have played gigs at the Moonlight Club, the Nashville, 100 Club, Hope and Anchor and Rock Garden, some of the most important club venues, and more are due.

These include a support slot to Talking Heads at the Electric Ballroom on 7 and 8 December, and gigs at the Bridge House, 11 December, Dingwalls, 14 December, and Windsor Castle, 15 December.

This should give the group a greater foothold in the rock establishment, in addition to their highly praised U-2-3 single on CBS Ireland and the fact that several major record companies across the channel have already shown interest in signing the band, no doubt encouraged by front page features in both *Hot Press* and *Record Mirror*.

Vol 3 No. 13 December 7th 1979.

●

U-2: "Another Day" (CBS)
THE OPENING bars may sound like others but there's no mistaking Bono's soaring entry – this band already know enough to

be different from the pack. They're committed, and ready to take a chance, so "Another Day" is champing, bright and blowing and overflowing with harmonic strength. There's a lot of love on this record – repay it.

Dermot Stokes, reviewing their second Irish single. Vol3 No. 18 Feb. 29, 1980.

●

Signing, of course, was heavily in the air where U-2 were concerned. With yet another deal imminent, and this time even more securely grasped than the others which all somehow seemed to slide away like a bar of soap just at the last minute, they knew that they were to some extent on trial. I'd previously only seen them in Dublin, and not since September at that, and at that stage I'd still felt that there were residual twinges of the Dublin disease, a slight lack of conviction, of urgency. Their stint here late last year has jettisoned any such quibbles this time around, however. Live at least, though not yet quite on record, they're now a fully rounded unit playing to, rather than against, their strengths.

Some of the music has been given a bit of a spring-clean too – for example the revised rhythm for "Stories For Boys". I still think there's something wrong with the internal dynamics of some of the songs; "Another Day", for instance, definitely loses pace in the middle. Bono is starting to move a little too much like the Ian Curtis/Numan school, but it's probably unintentional.

The Sense of Ireland gig in London, reviewed by Peter Owens. Vol 3 No. 20 March 29, 1980.

The U2 Way

1980. Bono writes about being in a band on the threshold.

Pic: Colm Henry

"Where were you last night?" asked the ol' man. "We played a concert in Trinity College." "How did it go?" "Well," I said, "we had a bit of trouble from a few 16 year olds in the audience." "You weren't very polite, yourself at sixteen!" he replied.

Yeh, I know at sixteen boys turn into men and get confused, I do remember. I remember I felt bullied by the need to succeed, to find a good job, and a pretty girl. Forming U2 was a way out — it was also a way in to expressing how I felt constructively, as opposed to banging my own or somebody else's head off a wall. The fact that neither Bono, Adam, Larry or the Edge could play or sing was but an obstacle to overcome. (It hadn't bothered Lou Reed, Bob Dylan or Bob Geldof). Just do it!

Dublin in 1977 was not as receptive to a new rock group with new rules as was London Town — the old story of Dublin living in the shadow, failing to make its own mind up. Even the music scene (man!) was loathe to jump up and down to what must have seemed like their little brothers. No, the group that sprayed "The Hype" on their Mount Temple comprehensive school-bags and shouted 1,2,3,4 at the Celebrity Club, were to say the least, a threat to one's cool. How dare they enjoy themselves.

A manager was needed before we learnt our next lesson. Paul McGuinness was his name and he wasn't very good at football! He told us not to over-expose

155

ourselves while we were still underdeveloped and not to rely on gigging and our status in Dublin (which wasn't very high at the time). He also arranged for Barry Devlin to produce our first demo and organised record company interest. Yes he's quite useful around the house! (in between sueing various non entities).

This was a foundation — it was up to the music to build the rest. Musically we were trying to combine the energy of the new wave with an added sensitivity and emotion. For this reason I feel we have more in common with, say, the Who than the Pistols or the Clash.

Progressing, though, is the name of the game and if you don't know how, then find someone who does. Myself and bass player Adam in particular sought as much advice as we could from both established musicians and music "biz" people. Stephen Rapid of Radiators fame was a great help, as were the three Bills, Bill Graham (*Hot Press*), Bil Keating (RTE) and Bill McGrath (Stagalee+ Atrix). Abroad, people like Johnnie Fingers, the Rats, the Lizzies were also glad to lend a hand. And we pushed a little too far: there was one incident where Adam got Phil Lynott out of his bed to answer a few questions about the universe. Philip was helpful but nobody's at their best at 7.30 am.! The point was and is "make allies before you make enemies".

Originality is the keyword. In terms of presentation, on stage, I try to catch people's attention, like an actor I try to get across the atmosphere of the words and the setting. Sometimes I fail, sometimes people don't want to know, sometimes I don't even know myself.

In the end it's up to you the audience to decide for yourselves, is it relevant or irrelevant, can you see the potential in U2 or not? So far you have decided yes and put our first record in the charts, "U2 three". Thank you.

Our debut tour in England was an incredible success; things look good for U2 and I feel confident that our February concert tour of all the major towns in Ireland will be successful too as, we also release our second single here then.

In March we undertake a second English tour in time for our first record release over there. Yes, it's an important time for me.

It's also time for tea! "What are you doing?" asks my ol' man. "I'm writing a piece for the *Hot Press*". "The who?", "A music paper". "How's it going?" he continued. "Well", I replied, "I had a bit of trouble ..." ∎

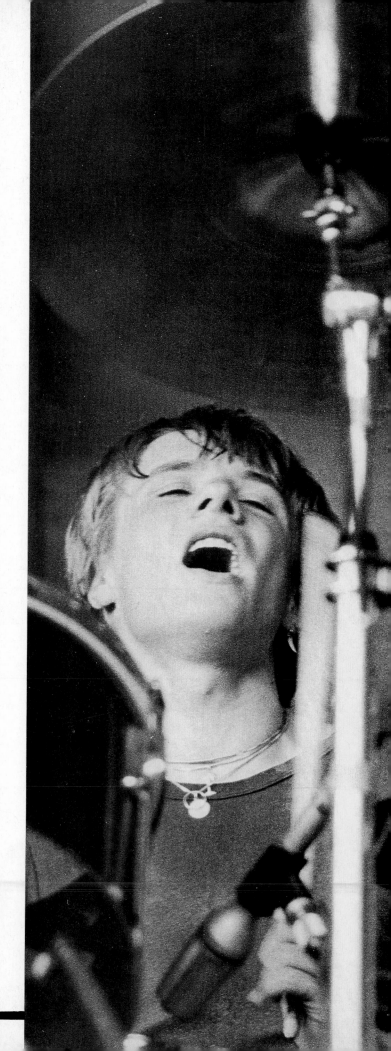

The beat behind the band. Pic: Colm Henry.

U-2: "A Day Without Me" (Island) and (CBS) D.C. NIEN: "Nightclub" (Nien-Teen Eight-Tease)

COMPARISONS can be odious. Both U-2 and D.C. Nien are presented according to their desires, neither need run to teacher with excuses and it should go without prompting from me that both of these are essential singles.

In U-2's case, their singles have tended to be less instantaneously dramatic than their live performances, requiring due patience before their musical curves are negotiated and the reward is gained. "A Day Without Me" doesn't have the spectral majesty of "11 O'Clock Tick Tock" but it is the closest portrayal yet of their giddy live rush.

Marked by an uncharacteristically jerky guitar signature from the Edge, U-2's wheels flash down a bumpier road than hitherto. Bono proclaims "I started a landslide in my ego" and his vocals sweep high into a starry-unclouded sky. Undoubtedly one further step for emotional positivism.

U-2's first international single, reviewed by Bill Graham. Vol 4 No. 4 August 14th 1980.

●

Following their current European stint, the band travel to the US for their first dates there. They then return to the States for a major assault on the popular consciousness first thing in the new year.

U-2's first album "Boy" has just been released to almost universal critical acclaim in Britain and Ireland. The British advance orders on the album numbered over 10,000 and, therefore, it is expected to chart strongly there either this week or next. Because of a delay in the delivery of the sleeve artwork from Island in Britain, CBS in Ireland have released the album *sans* jacket to satisfy the mounting demand. Hopefully, completed product will be on the shelves later this week.

News page, Vol 4 No. 11 October 24th 1980.

●

U-2: "I Will Follow" (CBS/Island)
Unlike Springsteen, these boys are in the first flush of youth, but there a lot of the contrasts end. What makes U-2 unique among their contemporaries is the extraordinary completeness of their vision. Where most young bands are over-defined by their environments and the trends and phases of music, U-2 have seen the life beyond.

The Edge. Pic: James Mahon.

Strength, commitment, energy, challenge, love, vision and completeness take this music out about and beyond the pack. And if this only the beginning, where will it end?

Almost unbelievable (provided they don't go for too much jesus). Meanwhile, I like the Steve Lillywhite production on this, surging power and deep bass and an increasingly confident vocal. Yeah, watch 'em go.

Dermot Stokes, Single Reviews, Vol 4 No. 13 November 21 1980.

●

SINGLE
1 U2: "11 O'Clock Tick Tock" (CBS)
2 U2: "A Day Without Me" (CBS)
3 Radiators: "Dancing Years" (Mulligan)
4 Paul Brady: "Crazy Dreams" (WEA)
5 The Atrix: "Treasure On The Wasteland (Double D)

BEST GROUP
1 U2
2 Boomtown Rats
3 Rory Gallagher
4 Undertones
5 Thin Lizzy

MALE SINGER
1 Bono
2 Paul Brady
3 Bob Geldof
4 Rory Gallagher
5 Feargal Sharkey

ALBUM
1 U2: "Boy" (CBS)
2 Undertones: "Hypnotized" (Sire)
3 Rory Gallagher: "Stagestruck"
4 Bagatelle: "Bagatelle" (Polydor)
5 Scullion: "Balance and Control" (WEA)

Readers Poll 1980, Vol 5 No. 1 January 1981

●

The winners of the Stag/Hot Press Irish Rock awards have just been announced and they are as follows ...

Best vocalist: Feargal Sharkey; Best Band: U-2; Best Live Band: U-2; Best Single: The Blades' "Ghost Of A Chance"; Best Album: U-2's "Boy"; Best Unrecorded Act: Chant! Chant!; Best Song: Paul Brady's "Crazy Dreams"; Best Musician: Rory Gallagher

The winners of the first Stag/Hot Press Rock Awards are announced. Vol 5 No. 12 June 26, 1981.

●

U-2: "Fire" (Island/CBS Double Single).

Just as U-2's career curve has constantly been in the ascendant over the last few years, so has their music travelled ever onward and upward — from the spirited but nervous "U23" through last year's accomplished debut album to the recently-recorded-live-for-US-radio album.

With "Fire" the dye is cast, the sword is drawn, the hammer cocked. Watch it fly from their heart to yours. A record to have and to hold, to dance and to play, in sickness and in health, in joy and in sorrow. The third and brightest, strongest most beautiful element. They broke the mould when they made U(2).

Ross Fitzsimons on singles Vol 5 No. 14 July 24 1981

Patrick Brocklebank.

157

The gig moved into an altogether different sphere with U-2. Starting with a piper onstage, and previewing several songs off the new LP, the band displayed yet again the power and joy of their music. Remarkable and original, emotive and responsive, dancing and singing, they communicated heart and soul with the crowd.

Supporting Thin Lizzy at Slane Castle, Vol 5 No. 16 August 21 1981

turn left at Greenland! Its like living in a Big Mac - But is it real meat? YEP its real meat, the french fries are plastic thankyou Neil. Good News travels slowly! It took a month to see the review, were fighting the Christmas rush of Greatest Bits etc We'll WIN the good guys always do in the end, Love Bono ringo george paul

ADDRESS
HOT PRESS
21 Upper Mount St.
Dublin, 2.
IRELAND

POST CARD

A postcard from The Fab Four to Hot Press during their first American tour.

Pic: Colm Henry.

Bono with Hazel O'Connor at Slane Castle, 1980.

U-2: "Gloria" (Island)

More U-2 chivalry as they surge forward with a track that could have featured in the soundtrack for "Excalibur". A knightly charge in pursuit of the Holy Grail, "Gloria" climaxes on the resounding re-entry of the chorus and De Edge's ardent guitar. Attend also to the B-side, a live recording of "I Will Follow" in Boston. Some consider live tracks to be duplication and false bait for the fans who must have everything but "I Will Follow" shows how U-2 buckle that particular rule.

Singles reviewed by Bill Graham Vol 5 No. 20 October 16th 1981

●

U-2: "Celebration" (Island)

"Who made the world? God made the world." Now I'm aware that we all live in little boxes and that we drink too much and back horses too much, but U-2's version of spiritual abandon harks back to the catechism — a few catch-phrases never freed a spider from his web. From Nottingham comes the word that the H.M. fraternity are smitten by The Edge's guitarwork on "Celebration". I like it but its charms

diminish as time goes by. U-2 might try to develop a few inhibitions.

Declan Lynch, Vol 6 No. 6 April 1, 1982.

●

In contrast, U-2 are a band whose collective star is still firmly in the ascendant — a state of affairs which is likely to continue as long as they retain their remarkable ability to communicate directly with their audience in a way that makes each one of their gigs an event unique unto itself.

A dissenting voice was sceptical of the band's intentions, claiming, in particular that Bono's exhortations from the stage can border on the mechanical. It's perhaps a thorny point and one that Bono may well want to answer for himself, but for my part, his overwhelming enthusiasm has little to do with stock rock manipulative routines and everything to do with a perfectly natural sense of joy derived from the making of exhilarating music.

And U-2's music *is* exhilarating. There are few bands anywhere these days who can match the passionate intensity that U-2 generate with songs like "Gloria", "A Day Without Me" and "I Will Follow".

Heart-warming and soul-inspiring, the U-2 fire burns on ...

Liam Mackey, Hot Press 5th Birthday gig Vol 6 No. 13. July 30 1982.

●

U-2: "New Year's Day" (Island)

On first listen this seems a curious choice of a single, not having any easily digestible hooks as such, but after a few plays the overall feel of the song hits home. A passionate performance with a lovely piano line drifting through the mix. However if the brilliant "Celebration" didn't set the UK

charts ablaze it'll be interesting to see how this does. Fingers crossed.

John Byrne on singles Vol 7 No. 1 January 21, 1983.

●

U-2: "Two Hearts Beat As One" (Island/CBS)

By now, this will be familiar to almost all of you, and rightly so. A loud, proud, warm love song recorded with true spirit and energy by "the Dublin four-piece". For me, its strongest components are Larry's brash drums and Bono's all-out vocals, both relentlessly lifting me higher and higher and forcing me back to the turntable time and again.

Mind you, I can't work out whether U-2 are actually making better records now or the world has finally woken up to them.

Ross Fitzsimons Vol 7 No. 7, April 15th 1983

1980. Larry models the magazine! Pic: Colm Henry.

The Edge and wife Aisling. Pic: Colm Henry.

HAVING ENTERED the British Charts at No. 8, last week U-2's "Pride In The Name Of Love" has risen to No. Three, suggesting that the band may top the singles charts for the first time.

The remarkable success of "Pride In The Name Of Love" comes at a crucial point in U-2's career. With a new album "Unforgettable Fire" scheduled to hit the shops in the first week of October, the feeling now is that the band have made the final leap into The Big League — their previous highest singles placing was with "New Years Day" which reached No. Ten.

If this success is repeated on a worldwide scale, as seems likely, U-2 will clearly have achieved an unassailable and well-deserved position of status and popularity — reaping full rewards for the committed stance they've adopted from the outset.

They've come a long way since the Dandelion Market!

Vol 8 No. 19, October 5th, 1984.

Bono with wife Ali in Ethiopia, September 1985

FEBRUARY 14th VALENTINE'S DAY
TODAY IS St. Valentine's Day and where is my Valentine? On the drive from Austin to San Antonio we stopped off at a snake farm/amateur zoo. It was very depressing. Lots of caged animals not looking very healthy. The high point was a mad monkey which had epileptic fits accompanied by blood-chilling shrieks. It was really quite a scream because Bono started singing. This infuriated the creature even further — its shrieks grew louder. Bono matched its volume until the deranged creature started to beat his head against the wall. Eventually a very brusque woman ran over and dismissed us, complaining how cruel it was to drink sodas in front of our friend as there was nothing it liked more than a glass of Coke.

On to the gig. During the show, Bono handed out flowers to girls. Wish I'd done that. He's got friends for life. Afterwards we spent a long time with the punters. The Texans are a nice simple people, consequently conversation lasted long. 3.15 a.m. back to the hotel via The Alamo, which received the dubious accolade of consecration with Ozzy Osbourne's urine.

"Fort Apache, the Bronx" was on the H.B.O. cable. Great film and Paul Newman's best performance in years.

FRIDAY
UP TOO early with everyone looking wrecked. Arrive in Denver and Edge discovers a ski resort 50 miles up country. The four of us head off. It had to be hushed up as a broken leg at this stage of the tour would not be welcome. Stories were fabricated and changed so that no-one had any idea where we were. It was a lovely drive through the Rockies to the resort. Once there, Edge organises the activities, as he is the experienced amateur. We get our skis on and Bono falls over immediately. We potter about on the nursery slopes under Edge's instructions. I eventually feel confident enough to try my luck on the mountain. I wish I hadn't. I've never been so frightened in all my life. To reach the top of the mountain we have to hang on a chair lift, hundreds of feet above the ground with no safety bar. I was so hysterical I would have gladly thrown myself off had Edge not kept me talking.

At the top it soon becomes obvious that I had been over optimistic. I tell Edge to go off and enjoy himself. I'll walk down. The mountain very nearly claimed me. Edge goes up and down twice in the time it takes me to walk. Then he did a black slope. As you might know black slopes are very serious. And then some, like black holes and black belts. We retire to the bar for the only bit of ski I like — apres ski and Gluewein. We make the mistake of ordering Irish Coffees, which are barely coffee and certainly not Irish. The cream comes from one of those aerosol jobs and there's a nasty green mint liqueur to boot. Once back in the hotel we decide to go and see REDS. It's a good film but I felt it lost its punch in places, but maybe that's because I was so tired.

Extracts from Adam Clayton's tour diary, Hot Press Vol 6 No. 14 August 1982.

Bono, Bob and Van

Bono: When you're working with a producer, do you give him that lee-way to challenge you?

Bob: Yeah, if he feels like it. But usually we just go into the studio, and sing a song, and play the music, and have, you know ...

Bono: Have you had somebody in the last five years who said "that's crap Bob".

Bob: Oh, they say that all the time!

Bono: Mark Knopfler, did he say that?

Bob: I don't know ...they spend time getting their various songs right, but with me, I just take a song into the studio and try to rehearse it, and then record it, and then do it. It's a little harder now though to make a good record — even if you've got a good song and a good band. Even if you go in and record it live, it's not gonna sound like it used to sound, because the studios now are so modern, and overly developed, that you take anything good and you can press it and squeeze it and squash it, and constipate it and suffocate it. You do a great performance in the studio and you listen back to it, it even sounds good when you listen back to it because the speakers are all so good, but, ah, no!

Bono: All technology does is — you go into a dead room with dead instruments and you use technology to give it life that it doesn't have, and then it comes out on the speakers and you believe it. What I've been trying to do is find a room that has life in itself.

Bob: Yeah.

Bono: A *living* room.

Bob: The machines though, can even take the life out of that room, I've found. You can record it in St. Peters Cathedral, you know, and they still make it sound like, eh ...

Bono: Somebody's back yard.

Bob: Yeah.

Bono: That's a good idea, I'd love to record in a cathedral.

Bob: You know the studios in the old days were all much better, and the equipment so much better, there's no question about it in my mind. You just walked into a studio — they were just big rooms. You just sang, you know, you just made records — and they sounded like the way they sounded there. That stopped happening in the late sixties, for me anyway, I noticed the big change. You go into a studio now, and they got rugs on the floors, settees, and pinball machines and videos and sandwiches coming every ten minutes — it's a big expensive party and you're lucky if you come out with *anything* that sounds decent.

Bono: Yeah, records haven't got better, have they?

Bob: No, you go in now, and you got your

Bono with a Hot Press Poll Award 1980.

producer, you got your engineer, you got your assistant engineer, usually your assistant producer, you got a guy carrying the tapes around. I mean, you know, there's a million people go into recording just an acoustic song on your guitar. The boys turn the machines on and it's a great undertaking.

Bono: There's a system called Effanel which Mick Fleetwood from Fleetwood Mac brought to Africa. It was built for him because he wanted to get some real African drumming, for "Tusk". We've used that system. It comes in a light suitcase, very small, no bullshit studio, and it just arrives, you can literally bring it to your living room.

Van: I think all the same they'll go back to 2-track eventually.

Bono: There's a guy called Conny Plank, who produced Makem and Clancy and some Irish traditional bands, also orchestral and funnily enough a lot of the new

U2 and Coconuts during the recording of "War".

electronic groups, DAF, Ultravox, and so on. He used to record orchestras by just finding a position in the room where they were already balanced and he applies this in his thinking, in recording modern music: he finds a place in the room where it's already mixed.

Van: I don't know, when I started we didn't think about that! You didn't even think about recording (*laughter*).

Bono: You didn't even think?

Van: You didn't even know what was on the cards. One day you were in the room, they turned the tape on. After about eight hours or so, they'd say "OK tea break, it's over".

Bob: Yeah, next song, next song!

Van: And then that was that — it was an album.

Bob: Yeah, you'd make an album in three days or four days and it was all over — if that many! It's that long now, it takes four days to get a drum sound!

Bono: Do you know the Monty Python team, they're comedians, British comedians, "Monty Python And The Holy Grail". They have a sketch that reminds me of you guys – sitting back talking of days gone by: "you tell that to the young people of today and they'd never believe you". But you can't go backwards, you must go forward. You try to bring the values that were back there, you know, the strength, and if you see something that was lost, you've got to find a new way to capture that same strength. Have you any ideas on how to do that? I think you've done it by the way ... I think "Shot Of Love" that opening track has got that.

Bob: I think so too. (*drawls*). You're one of the few people to say that to me about that record, to mention that record to me.

Bono: That has *that* feeling.

Bob: It's a great record, it suits just about everybody.

Bono: The sound from that record ("Shot Of Love") makes me feel like I'm in the same room as the other musicians — I don't feel that they're *over there*. Some of our records, I feel like they're over there because we got into this cinema-type sound, not bland like FM sound, but we got into this very *broad* sound. Now we're trying to focus more of a punch, and that's what we are after, this intimacy ... I've never interviewed anybody before, by the way. I hate being interviewed myself.

Van: You're doing a good job!

Bono: Is this OK? God!

Bono talking with Bob Dylan and Van Morrison.
Hot Press, Vol 8 No. 16 August 24th, 1984.

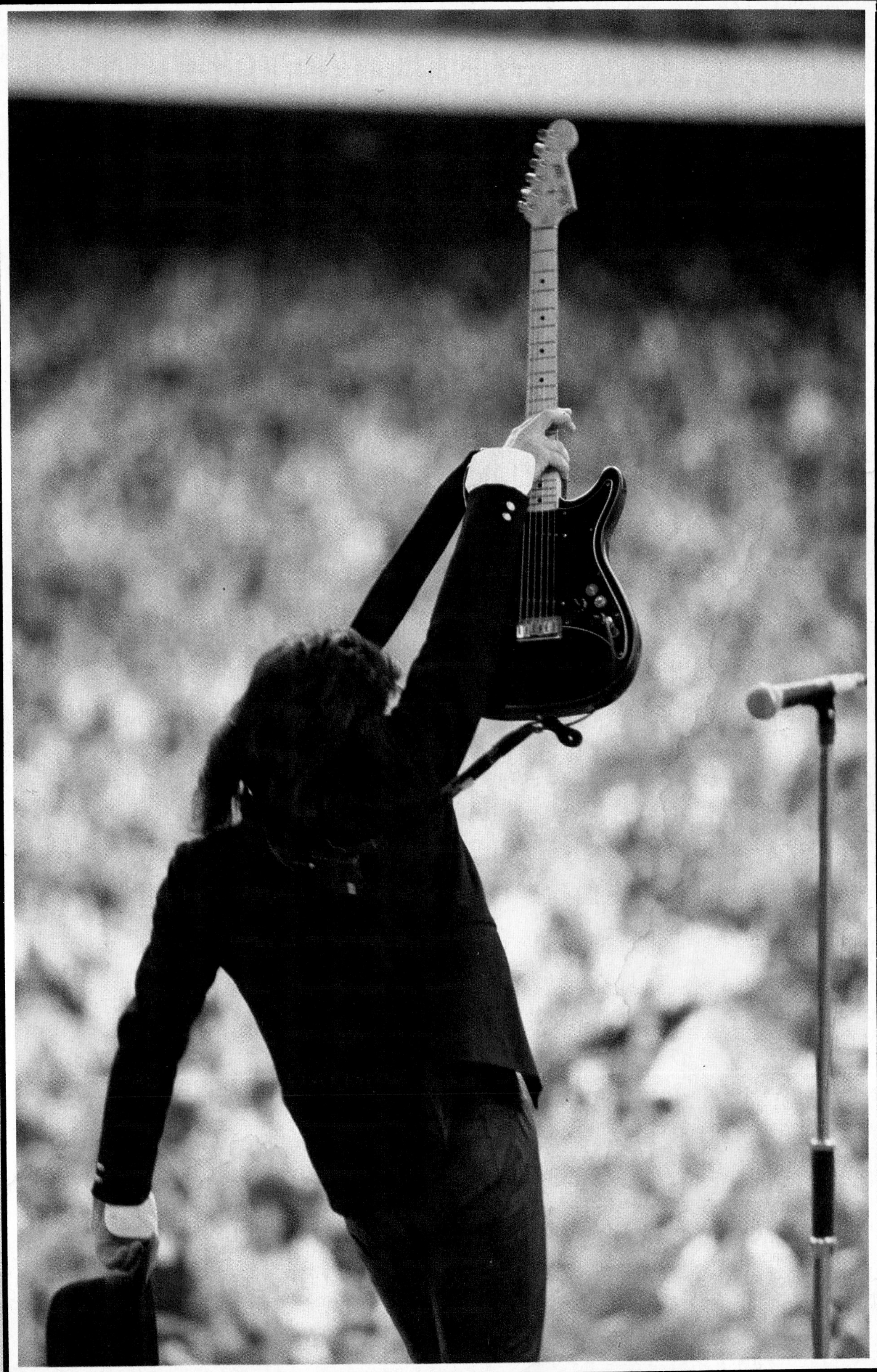

Pic: Colm Henry.

Discography

SINGLES

"U23" E.P. (CBS Irl)

Producer:	Chas de Whalley and U2
Tracks:	Out Of Control/Boy-Girl/Stories For Boys
Format:	12" (1000 numbered copies) 7" (Pic. Sleeve)
Released:	September 1979

"ANOTHER DAY" (CBS Irl)

Producer:	Chas de Whalley and U2
B-Side:	Twilight
Format:	7" (Pic. Sleeve)
Released:	February 1980

"11 O'CLOCK TICK TOCK" (Island)

Producer:	Martin Hannett
B-Side:	Touch
Format:	7" (Pic. Sleeve)
Released:	May 1980

"A DAY WITHOUT ME" (Island)

Producer:	Steve Lillywhite
B-Side:	Things To Make And Do
Format:	7" (Pic. Sleeve)
Released:	August 1980

"I WILL FOLLOW" (Island)

Producer:	Steve Lillywhite
B-Side:	Boy-Girl (Live)
Format:	7" (Pic. Sleeve)
Released:	October 1980

"FIRE" (Island)

Producer:	Steve Lillywhite
B-Side:	J Swallow
Format:	7" Double-Pack (Gatefold Pic. Sleeve); also features Live versions of 11 O'Clock Tick Tock/The Ocean/Cry/The Electric Co.
Released:	July 1981

"GLORIA" (Island)

Producer:	Steve Lillywhite
B-Side:	I Will Follow (Live)
Format:	7" (Pic. Sleeve)
Released:	October 1981

"A CELEBRATION" (Island)

Producer:	Steve Lillywhite
B-Side:	Trash Trampoline And The Party Girls
Format:	7" (Pic. Sleeve)
Released:	March 1982

"NEW YEAR'S DAY" (Island)

Producer:	Steve Lillywhite
B-Side:	Treasure (Whatever Happened To Pete The Chop)
Format:	7" (Pic. Sleeve); 12" features live versions of Fire/I Threw A Brick/A Day Without Me
Released:	January 1983

"TWO HEARTS BEAT AS ONE" (Island)

Producer:	Steve Lillywhite
B-Side:	Endless Deep
Format:	7" Double-Pack (Gatefold Pic. Sleeve) features Two Hearts (remix)/New Year's Day (remix); 12" Club Mix featuring Two Hearts/Endless Deep/New Year's Day
Released:	March 1983

"PRIDE (In The Name Of Love)" (Island)

Producer:	Brian Eno and Daniel Lanois
B-Side:	Boomerang II
Format:	7" (Pic. Sleeve); 12" features Boomerang I/Boomerang II/4th Of July
Released:	September 1984

"THE UNFORGETTABLE FIRE" (Island)

Producer:	Brian Eno and Daniel Lanois
B-Side:	A Sort Of Homecoming
Format:	7" and Double-Pack (Gatefold Pic. Sleeve) features Love Comes Tumbling/60 Seconds In Kingdom Come/3 Sunrises
Released:	May 1985

All titles available on CBS Records in Republic of Ireland

"WIDE AWAKE IN AMERICA"
American EP (Island)

Producer:	Tony Visconti (A Sort Of Homecoming);U2/Eno/Lanois (The Three Sunrises); U2 (Love Comes Tumbling); "Bad" mixed by Ron St. Jermain
Tracks:	Bad/A Sort Of Homecoming (Live)/The Three Sunrises/Love Comes Tumbling
Format:	12" (Pic. Sleeve)
Recorded:	American Tour 84 - 85; Slane Castle, Co. Meath; Windmill Lane, Dublin
Released:	May 1985

ALBUMS

"BOY" (Island)

Track Listing:

Side 1:	I Will Follow/Twilight/An Cat Dubh/Into The Heart/Out Of Control
Side 2:	Stories For Boys/The Ocean/A Day Without Me/Another Time, Another Place/The Electric Co/Shadows And Tall Trees
Producer:	Steve Lillywhite
Recorded:	Windmill Lane, Dublin
Released:	October 1980

"OCTOBER" (Island)

Track Listing:

Side 1:	Gloria/I Fall Down/I Threw A Brick Through A Window/Rejoice/Fire
Side 2:	Tomorrow/October/With A Shout/Stranger In A Strange Land/Scarlet/Is That All?
Producer:	Steve Lillywhite
Recorded:	Windmill Lane, Dublin
Released:	October 1981

"WAR" (Island)

Track Listing:

Side 1:	Sunday Bloody Sunday/Seconds/New Year's Day/Like A Song . . ./Drowning Man
Side 2:	The Refugee/Two Hearts Beat As One/Red Light/Surrender/"40"
Producer:	Steve Lillywhite (The Refugee produced by Bill Whelan and mixed by Lillywhite)
Recorded:	Windmill Lane, Dublin
Released:	March 1983

"UNDER A BLOOD RED SKY" (Island)

Track Listing:

Side 1:	Gloria/11 O'Clock Tick Tock/I Will Follow/Party Girl
Side 2:	Sunday Bloody Sunday/The Electric Co/New Year's Day/"40"
Producer:	Jimmy Iovine
Recorded:	Boston, Denver and West Germany
Released:	November 1983

"THE UNFORGETTABLE FIRE" (Island)

Track Listing:

Side 1:	A Sort Of Homecoming/Pride (In The Name Of Love)/Wire/The Unforgettable Fire/Promenade
Side 2:	4th Of July/Bad/Indian Summer Sky/Elvis Presley And America/MLK
Producer:	Brian Eno and Daniel Lanois
Recorded:	Slane Castle, Co. Meath; Windmill Lane, Dublin
Released:	October 1984